# TRAUMA and the AVOIDANT CLIENT

A NORTON PROFESSIONAL BOOK

# TRAUMA and the AVOIDANT CLIENT

*Attachment-Based Strategies for Healing*

Robert T. Muller

W. W. Norton & Company, Inc.
New York • London

Printed in the United States of America
First Edition

For information about permission to reproduce selections from this book, write to Permissions, W. W. Norton & Company, Inc., 500 Fifth Avenue, New York, NY 10110

For information about special discounts for bulk purchases, please contact W. W. Norton Special Sales at specialsales@wwnorton.com or 800-233-4830

Manufacturing by R.R. Donnelley, Bloomsburg
Production manager: Leeann Graham

Library of Congress Cataloging-in-Publication Data

Muller, Robert T.
Trauma and the avoidant client : attachment-based strategies for healing / Robert T. Muller.—1st ed.
p. ; cm.
"A Norton Professional Book."
Includes bibliographical references and index.
ISBN 978-0-393-70573-7 (hardcover)
1. Psychic trauma. 2. Avoidance (Psychology) 3. Attachment behavior. I. Title. [DNLM: 1. Stress Disorders, Post-Traumatic—therapy. 2. Denial (Psychology) 3. Life Change Events. 4. Object Attachment. 5. Psychotherapy—methods. WM 170 M9469t 2010]
RC552.T7M85 2010
616.85'21—dc22

2009052115

ISBN: 978-0-393-70573-7

W. W. Norton & Company, Inc., 500 Fifth Avenue, New York, N.Y. 10110
www.wwnorton.com
W. W. Norton & Company Ltd., Castle House, 75/76 Wells Street, London W1T 3QT

6 7 8 9 0

To
Diane

And to
Aviva, Aaron, and Noah

For the love, inspiration, and joy they have given

# Contents

# Acknowledgments

There are many people who have helped make this book a reality. I credit my treatment approach to the supervision and readings I was exposed to early on in my training. As an undergraduate research assistant for Dr. David Bakan, I first became interested in the field of trauma and psychotherapy. And, as a graduate student in the mid-1980s, I soon imprinted on psychodynamic psychotherapy at Michigan State University, where Dr. Bertram Karon's directive approach with very high-risk clients taught me to formulate and work within a psychodynamic framework that engages the individual, builds hope, and values the therapeutic relationship. The writings of Dr. Lester Luborsky (1984) and Dr. David Malan (e.g., 1979/1995) figured heavily into my training at that time. Later, during my postdoctoral fellowship at Harvard University and Massachusetts General Hospital, my clinical supervisors at the time, Dr. Robert Reifsnyder and Dr. Steven Nisenbaum, taught me to formulate within an attachment-based framework. Soon after, the publication of Dr. Judith Herman's *Trauma and Recovery* in 1992 made a lasting impression on my approach to treatment with survivors of trauma.

I am grateful for the ideas, insights, and feedback that I have received from my colleagues and peers. Dr. Lynn Angus at York University, and Dr. Charles Gelso, editor of the scholarly journal *Psychotherapy*, provided valuable feedback on the earlier articles on which this book was based. My wife (and colleague) Dr. Diane Philipp spent long hours reading and editing multiple drafts of the book manuscript, as did associate editor Andrea Costella at W. W. Norton. I also benefited enormously from the editorial insights of Dr. Daniel Carlat, publisher and editor of the *Carlat Psychiatry Report,* and from Steven Muller, L.L.M., who provided a detailed, comprehensive review of the manuscript. In addition, I would like to thank my friends and colleagues of many years, Dr. Peter Snyder and Dr. Christopher Green, for their insight and guidance regarding the academic book-publishing process. And, I thank Natalie Zlodre, M.S.W., at the Hincks-Dellcrest Centre, for her suggestion several years ago that I put together clinical workshops on the topic of trauma and avoidance and for her helpful guidance in that process.

I am grateful for my graduate students Kristin Gragtmans, Julie Cinamon, Karina Zorzella, Susan Rosenkranz, Ritu Bedi, Cheryl Fernandes, and Lise McLewin for their love of learning, their dedication, and their energetic commitment to this area of research. Thanks also to Adele Newcombe and Zohrah Haqanee who helped find some of the articles used in the literature review.

I would also like to express my gratitude to my clients. I am not sure they realize just how much they have taught me over the years.

Finally, this book is dedicated to my wife, Diane, and to my children, Aviva, Aaron, and Noah. Their love and support have been boundless and unwavering.

# TRAUMA and the AVOIDANT CLIENT

# Introduction

> I don't want to *pretend*, I don't want to take part in the grand social conspiracy that makes widows tell strangers on the bus that "it was his time," or makes parents of buried children say, "Well, we're just happy we had her for as long as we did," or that in any other way makes any of us pretend that we're not furious about the double-edged broadsword of life and death. (Scott Peck, *All-American Boy*, 1995, p. 91)

This book begins with a few simple questions. How do you engage the client who pretends, the client who denies and minimizes the effects of her own cruel past? How do you help the vulnerable individual who cannot admit to her own vulnerabilities? How do you work with the trauma survivor who is not so sure that she wants to be helped?

For the clinician who is seeking a therapeutic connection, who is attempting to engage the client, there is no question that such a person is hard to treat. In fact, it may be tempting instead to write off individuals such as these as "treatment resistant" or to refer them to others. Perhaps this, in part, is why the development of specific intervention strategies for this clinical population has been rather slow moving. Although there is much written about the frustrations of working with such clients, there is far less that can actually be used as a practical guide to treatment.

Earlier in my career, when I was still on faculty at the University of Massachusetts, I attended a talk delivered by a colleague at a meeting of the Society for Family Therapy and Research. Higgins (1994a) described her findings on a group of resilient adults who had managed to overcome the effects of their traumatic histories. I was so intrigued by this talk that the topic of resilience among trauma survivors came to shape my earlier academic interests. A positive sense of the human spirit can be inspiring. However, as I did more and more clinical work with adults who had experienced intrafamilial trauma and as I received training in attachment theory and assessment, I came to realize that the story is actually much more complicated than I had previously thought: A good many trauma survivors *pretend* to be doing a lot better than they really are. They pretend for years on end. They pretend for others, and they pretend for themselves. And, the individual who pretends to be okay (but who is otherwise in need of help) *is* in fact hard to treat.

This book is about the psychotherapy of trauma. Attachment-related traumatic experiences, intrafamilial abuse or neglect, and traumatic losses are the primary traumatic stressors considered.[1] In each of the cases presented, an important trust has been violated. Thus, fundamental to this work is the development of a strong therapeutic alliance to ultimately help the client regain a sense of trust in others. The treatment approach is attachment oriented and psychodynamic. It uses the therapeutic relationship as a means of understanding the individual's relational difficulties and compensatory mechanisms. The client is encouraged to take interpersonal risks, to express feelings he would normally keep buried, to mourn losses, to face his vulnerabilities. A lot of personal digging is asked of the clinician as well. One of the more dense chapters (Chapter 6) focuses on therapist countertransference. Treatment choices in this work are often mediated by the clinician's own attachment history and pattern of vulnerability.

But, this book is also different from others on the treatment of trauma. This book is about helping those who have learned to pretend. *Avoidant attachment* is characterized by the minimization of hurtful attachment experiences. When the avoidant client speaks of a given traumatic intrafamilial event, his tendency is to minimize the event's meaning or its perceived negative impact. Painful stories are discussed in an emotionally detached, intellectualized manner, often rationalized in one way or another or avoided altogether by focusing on other less-threatening material. Having developed a worldview that others cannot be depended on, the individual tends toward a pattern of self-reliance and a view of self as independent, strong, and normal. Along with this pattern, there is a tendency to dismiss and devalue experiences of closeness, intimacy, and vulnerability.

1. Note that I will *not* be concentrating on those traumatic experiences arising out of natural calamities, human-made disasters, traffic accidents, hijackings, terrorist attacks, and the like.

Given the tendency for clients in this population to be rather help rejecting, the treatment approach emphasizes ways to facilitate client engagement. It is important to find points of entry and ways to make contact. Conversations that encourage the client to clarify his various motivations for treatment can help the individual engage in, value, and use the therapeutic process. Throughout this book, I include strategies on how to develop and maintain client engagement in the treatment.

In our professional work, our biases tend to shape what we see. We are drawn toward clients and issues that touch a personal chord. My colleague of many years, C. Ward Struthers, has often described psychological *re*-search as psychological *me*-search. So, I would be lying if I characterized my interest in this population as deriving entirely from clinical or academic work. My parents grew up in Budapest. When Hungary was occupied during the last year of World War II, my parents were just school-aged children. They were separated from their families and, having been given falsified papers, were able to spend several months in hiding. They only survived the Holocaust through a combination of extraordinary luck and the goodwill of a few non-Jewish relatives who had married into my parents' otherwise large Jewish families.

For me, growing up as a child of "Holocaust survivors" meant hearing a lot of stories. Sometimes heartbreaking, always compelling, stories of the Holocaust were often recounted in my presence. It was only as a young adult that I came to realize that not all families with my background discussed their traumatic experiences of the Holocaust in the same way. Some shared their stories with their closest family members; others did not. Some never, ever talked about it. And, some felt such shame and disillusionment that they hid from their own children not only their traumatic experiences during the Holocaust, but also everything to do with their religious backgrounds and cultural identities.

In a poignant and moving article by writer John Lorinc (2008), the author described how his Hungarian father, who had been tortured in a forced labor camp, coped with his embitterment after the war by changing his nose and his Jewish-sounding surname. As a young child, Lorinc was baptized, he celebrated Christmas, and he knew nothing of his family's tragic history. Three years before his death, in a private father-son moment, Lorinc's father confessed that the family was, in fact, Jewish, quickly adding, "You mustn't tell anyone." Lorinc, who initially struggled to keep the family secret for many years, described his long, arduous journey to "come out" with respect to his Jewish identity.

> I began to realize that I had grown up in a Maranos-like environment—no public acknowledgement of Jewishness, but filled with the vestiges of that culture. (p. F10).

We make our way through this book as follows: In Chapter 1, through the lens of attachment theory, we begin to look at the defensive and interpersonal patterns seen among individuals in this clinical population. Next (Chapter 2), we consider a guiding approach for working with such clients, what research suggests in regard to challenging avoidant defenses, and why such intervention is, in principle, important and useful but in many ways demanding and difficult to navigate. Chapters 3 to 6 address the nuts and bolts of the treatment. In particular, Chapter 3 introduces the reader to focused intervention strategies that are necessary for the very early phases of therapy, strategies that help the clinician get started, for example, initially using symptoms as motivators for therapy but soon helping the client find other meaningful connections to the treatment process. Chapter 4 addresses emotional detachment and ways to facilitate the experience of mourning to help the client face the loss associated with trauma. Chapter 5 turns to the therapeutic relationship, to the difficulties that arise when attempting to connect empathically with clients in this population, how we can address such challenges, and how to use the relationship in the service of the therapy. In Chapter 6, with its focus on countertransference, therapist feelings in relation to the client are examined, along with many of the problematic ways the therapist may act on the feelings that get provoked in her through the course of therapy. Chapter 7 uses a case study to look at how the various intervention components may fit together. In the last section, Chapter 8, we consider the ending of therapy, along with strategies to reduce the problem of early termination.

I considered it important to make this book a practical, usable guide. Much has been produced over the years on the treatment of trauma. However, little has been written on specific strategies to help the traumatized client who is avoidant of attachment. With that in mind, I included practical case examples to illustrate clinical technique or therapeutic process.[2] Some of these examples show how the treatment might proceed well, but others demonstrate how

2. Throughout this book, the client is referred to as "he" or "she" interchangeably. All case studies are composites based on several actual clients.

things can go off track. Whenever I present this work at conferences, therapists express interest in case material that relates to their personal and professional struggles with these hard-to-treat clients. Therefore, the cases described in this book represent those scenarios that go well as well as those that are a struggle for the clinician.

Finally, throughout this book, in presenting the difficult aspects of working with this population, I have also attempted to describe specific ways to address those challenges and to facilitate change. My goal is that, on coming to the end, the reader will be both realistic and hopeful; will know what to expect but will be eager to apply the strategies learned.

# CHAPTER 1

# What Do Avoidant Defenses Look Like?

Let us begin with a clinical case study to illustrate how the avoidant client presents in treatment. The case of Sandra will help clarify the defensive and interpersonal patterns of individuals who have traumatic histories but who rely heavily on attachment avoidance as a means of coping. As we shall see, there is a tendency for such clients to retreat from psychological pain and vulnerability, using avoidance as a defense against traumatic distress.

---

*The Case of Sandra*

Sandra came to see me because she was finding it increasingly difficult to function effectively at work. Throughout her first session, it became clear that she was suffering from many of the classic symptoms of depression. She was often irritable and unhappy for reasons she could not understand. Her ability to concentrate was no longer what it used to be. Her friends had noticed that she rarely called them anymore and was not interested in going anywhere other than work. She reported this to be quite unusual for her because she always had been a "social butterfly," as she put it. Insomnia was another problem she identified, complaining that she was now staying up late into the night playing solitaire on her computer.

Despite having lived in the city for years and being well connected both socially and professionally, she found me not through word of mouth or referral from a family doctor but rather by way of an Internet search. Although commonplace now, when I saw her it was unusual for people to look for therapists using the Web. In reflecting on the case, it became clear to me that this was consistent with her overall state of loneliness and self-isolation at the time.

In our first meeting, when the question of important early losses came up, Sandra denied having had any, stating that everything was always "pretty normal" in her family of origin. We were just about wrapping up the first session when she spontaneously asked me if nannies "counted." I inquired further, to which she responded flatly, "She died," evidently responding to my earlier question surrounding important early losses; however, she did not wish to elaborate much at that point.

The significance of this loss only became clear months later in therapy when I was to discover that up to middle childhood, her nanny was, in fact, the one most consistent adult in her life. When she was very young, Sandra's parents would spend most weekends and evenings away either entertaining clients or on lengthy trips. Her older brother later informed her that it was their nanny who had largely raised them, teaching them both how to ride their bicycles, swim, and read; however, Sandra could not recall any of this herself, and as an adult did not really believe him until he reminded her that for months she was badly teased by other children at school for reading aloud with a Jamaican accent (her nanny had come from Jamaica).

During one weekend when her parents were away on business, the nanny was found dead by Sandra, who stayed with the body for almost 2 days, to be discovered only on her parents' return. A number of details suggested that the death was probably a suicide, likely witnessed by Sandra. Again, this was a story told to her by her brother years after the event as Sandra had little memory of her own or of very much else prior to age 10. Early in therapy, when asked about her feelings regarding this loss, she would look away, shrug her shoulders, and generally dismiss the importance of the event, responding in a matter-of-fact manner, with cool equanimity, "It was no biggie . . . next question?" as well as, "Look, stuff happens!"

## John Bowlby and Attachment Theory

Sandra's story will be instructive in coming to understand the kind of client who is the focus of this book. The theoretical framework driving our approach is that of attachment theory. Long considered a pioneer in the field, John Bowlby (1980, 1988) based his understanding largely on evolutionary theory and ethology. Bowlby considered the tendency to form attachment relationships as representing survival value in humans. He conceived of the attachment behavioral system as a biologically based system oriented toward seeking protection and maintaining proximity to the attachment figure in response to real or perceived threat or danger. Even when the attachment figure provides suboptimal caregiving, the developing child does what is necessary to maintain the primary attachment relationship. In such circumstances, the child gradually develops stable patterns of defense and affect regulation that "adapt" to the caregiving context (Bowlby, 1988). In other words, children will psychologically adapt to their primary relationships to survive in the environment in which they live. Therefore, even attachment patterns considered "insecure" may have been realistic adaptations when they occurred within a particular caregiving environment (Crittenden, 1999). It is only when the strategies inherent in the insecure attachment patterns are subsequently rigidly applied to new contexts and situations that they may be viewed as maladaptive (Daniel, 2006). Thus, to the extent that clients with histories of intrafamilial trauma have experienced extraordinary violations of interpersonal trust, difficulty trusting others may serve a purpose for a time but may become a liability as far as the development of new relationships is concerned.

Bowlby (1980) strongly emphasized the importance of lived experiences in child–caregiver interactions and in the subsequent development of basic affective, cognitive, and behavioral functioning. He posited that internal working models grow from repeated experiences with the primary caregiver through which children start to develop expectations about how future attachment-related interactions will operate (Main, Kaplan, & Cassidy, 1985).

Different patterns of adult attachment are presumed to follow from the working models that developed during childhood and adolescence. Research on these patterns of adult attachment has been heavily influenced by the development of the Adult Attachment Interview (AAI; George, Kaplan, & Main,

1996; see Hesse, 1999, for a review). In this interview, the participant is asked to respond to questions designed to activate the attachment system, such as questions about early separations, parental responses to childhood distress or illness, significant losses or abuse, instances of parental rejection, and so on.

Unique patterns of adult attachment have been described in the developmental research literature. Adults said to be *autonomous* (secure) coherently present a balanced, consistent, and objective view of early relationships, whether the experiences being discussed were favorable or not. They value attachment relationships as influential in their development. In contrast, insecure attachments include those individuals who are *avoidant* (also referred to as *dismissing*) of attachment-related experiences and relationships. They demonstrate discomfort with the discussion of such experiences, deny the impact of early attachment relationships on their development, have difficulty recalling specific childhood events, minimize or downplay difficult feelings associated with attachment experiences, and often idealize or derogate one or both caregivers. *Preoccupied* individuals—also insecure—are preoccupied with or by past attachment relationships and experiences, often appearing angry, fearful, or passive. Their speech patterns are characterized by long, rambling discussions, irrelevant material, lapses into expression of current anger at the caregiver in question, and childlike speech. Finally, individuals demonstrating the *unresolved* pattern show striking lapses in the monitoring of reasoning or discourse when loss or trauma are discussed, for example, a momentary belief that a dead person is still alive in the physical sense (Hesse, 1999). Unresolved attachment patterns may co-occur with any of the others and are often seen in conjunction with other patterns of attachment insecurity, such as avoidant or preoccupied attachment (Table 1.1).

## Defensive Exclusion

Let us now delve more deeply into an important aspect of attachment theory that can be helpful as we consider the nature of Sandra's difficulties, specifically Bowlby's (1980) concept of defensive exclusion. George and West (2004) have noted that despite its central place in theory, attachment researchers have paid relatively little attention to this concept.

Table 1.1
**Patterns of Adult Attachment and Their Main Features**

| | |
|---|---|
| *Secure (autonomous) attachment:* View of early relationships is coherent, balanced, consistent, and objective, whether experiences discussed were favorable or not. Values relationships as influential in own development. Demonstrates collaborativeness during attachment interview. | *Avoidant (dismissing) attachment:* Insecure pattern. Describes early relationships in an inconsistent, imbalanced way, minimizing or downplaying painful feelings associated with attachment experiences, often idealizing or derogating one or both caregivers; demonstrates discomfort with the discussion of attachment experiences; denies the impact of early attachment relationships on own development; has difficulty recalling specific childhood events; normalizes negative childhood events. |
| *Preoccupied attachment:* Insecure pattern. Early relationships described in inconsistent, imbalanced way. Individual demonstrates preoccupation with past attachment relationships and experiences, with such discussions taking on tone of anger, conflict, fear, or passivity. Speech patterns characterized by long, rambling discussions, irrelevant material, lapses into expression of anger at the caregiver in question or at current partner, and use of pseudopsychological jargon. | *Unresolved attachment:* Individual shows striking lapses in the monitoring of reasoning or discourse when loss or trauma are being discussed, for example, a momentary belief that a dead person is still alive in the physical sense (Hesse, 1999). This pattern is considered to co-occur with any of the others and is often seen in conjunction with other patterns of attachment insecurity, such as preoccupied or avoidant attachment. |

*Note:* Much of the material in this table is taken from the work of Main and Hesse (see Hesse, 1999).

Drawing on theory and research in the areas of psychoanalysis as well as human information processing (e.g., Dixon, 1971; Erdelyi, 1974; Hilgard, 1973, 1974; Norman, 1976; Peterfreund, 1971; Tulving, 1972), Bowlby (1980) held that sensory inflow goes through many stages of selection, interpretation, and appraisal before it can influence behavior, and that some information is excluded from processing, so that experiences or feelings that should be attended to as signals are transformed into unintegrated noise.

In the typical course of life, much information is routinely excluded from conscious processing so that capacities are not overloaded and the individual is not overly distracted. However, information that is *defensively excluded* is of the kind that, when accepted for processing in the past, has led the person to experience considerable suffering. Bowlby (1980) saw the process of defensive exclusion as arising from certain distressing attachment-related experiences. As an example, he considered the case in which the child's attachment behavior is strongly aroused but is responded to inadequately by the parent. Normally, in response to perceived threat or danger, the child seeks closeness or protection from caregivers. But, if the parental response is one of active rejection, threats, or severe punishment, the child will feel prolonged distress rather than feeling soothed. When this kind of parental response recurs frequently or for long periods, the child comes to exclude information that would normally activate attachment-related behaviors, with the resulting state one of emotional detachment.

Defensive exclusion also comes about from those circumstances in which the child observes aspects of a parent's behavior that the parent would prefer the child not know about (Bowlby, 1980). Some parents are highly insistent that their children regard them in a favorable light, and many children feel explicit or implicit pressure to turn a blind eye to adverse parental treatment, such as rejection or maltreatment, or to find a way to justify harsh parenting as a response to child misbehavior. Bowlby observed that in treatment, there is often a conflict between the client's favorable image of the parent and the unflattering reality, and that information that does not fit with the favorable image is defensively excluded.

This last aspect of defensive exclusion has been used in research on the AAI (George et al., 1996; Hesse, 1999) to code for instances of idealization of one or both parents, a phenomenon often observed in individuals avoidant of attachment. *Idealization* refers to general characterizations of the parent that come across as far more positive than the specific recalled events warrant (e.g., "My mother was *caring* because she only spanked us in private, never in public" [emphasis added]). In her book on recovery from trauma, Herman (1992) described the tendency to idealize one or both parents in families in which children have been victimized. She considered idealization to be a desperate attempt to preserve faith in one's parents. Herman went on to observe that it is common for the child to idealize the abusive parent, displacing all rage onto the nonoffending one. In such a process, the individual shields the maltreating parent from criticism and channels feelings of hurt and anger in the direction of the nonoffending parent because it is safe to do so. Any such expressions of hurt, criticism, or anger toward the perpetrator might be thought of as dangerous to oneself, with potential to destroy the relationship.

In contrast, idealization can also occur in the opposite direction, with the abusive parent viewed with criticism, while the nonoffending one is idealized, even put up on a pedestal or seen as a martyr of sorts. Although the latter may have failed to protect the child, failed to create conditions of safety in the home, or even enabled many of the hurtful actions carried out by others, in comparison to the maltreating parent, the nonoffending one may be seen as the lifeline, the one providing relative safety in an environment that was physically or psychologically dangerous. Hence, that parent may be viewed in idealized terms, and any feelings of hurt, anger, or ambivalence are buried. It is important to note that in both instances of parental idealization, the psychological process is similar. Critical information is defensively excluded in a desperate attempt to manage personal safety and to preserve a positive image and faith in one or both parents.

In describing defensive exclusion, Bowlby (1980) considered it from an evolutionary standpoint, noting that the question was whether it promoted survival. He made use of observations described by Main (1977) of infant behavior during the experimental paradigm, the strange situation (Ainsworth & Bell, 1970; Ainsworth & Wittig, 1969). In this paradigm, the infant was exposed to increasingly stressful separations from the primary caregiver, typically the mother, and by observing the infant's behavior on reunion, a coding system was developed to categorize infants into attachment subtypes. During these observations, some infants, regarded as habitually rejected by their mothers, turned away from them on reunion, failing to greet them, failing to look at them, or tending to crawl away. Despite being in a strange setting, the child's response to the parent was one of avoidance, focusing attention instead on the available toy. In doing so, the child was reducing the risk of being rejected and minimizing the distress accompanying such rejection. Yet, the child remained in the mother's vicinity. Bowlby and Main explained that the avoidant response allows for a survival strategy different from seeking closeness to the caregiver. It allows the child to avoid the negative emotional state associated with closeness to a rejecting parent, yet it also means remaining near enough to the caregiver who represents the child's best odds for survival should there be an external danger.

Thus, Bowlby (1980) considered the defensive exclusion of information to be explainable in evolutionary terms given certain adverse circumstances. When such mental operations exclude information from awareness, painful emotions and memories are avoided. Feelings such as fear and anger may be shut off at key points in time, such as, say, when there is a threat of loss or separation (Sable, 2004).

## Avoidant Defenses

Clients such as Sandra have considerable difficulty with many aspects of the interpersonal world in part because of a powerful tendency to defensively exclude attachment-related information and experiences from awareness or to exclude the emotional meaning of such experiences. This tendency was particularly apparent when Sandra was asked about early attachment experiences. That is, she would rely heavily on *deactivation* as a defensive strategy. By shifting attention away from events or feelings that arouse the attachment system, individuals avoid difficult emotion and evade memories of painful relationship episodes with caregivers. Bowlby (1980) proposed that, through deactivation, information of significance to the individual can be systematically excluded from further processing, likening the concept of deactivation to that of repression. In their research on child and adult attachment, George and colleagues (George & Solomon, 1996; George & West, 2001; Solomon, George, & De Jong, 1995) demonstrated that the main distinguishing features of the avoidant pattern of attachment is the tendency to use deactivation as a defensive strategy.[3]

By deactivating attachment, the client shifts attention away from memories of potentially painful relationship episodes with caregivers (George & West, 2001, 2004), thereby avoiding possible threat to the relationship or to the individual's view of the relationship. In Bowlby's (1988) view, this was "avoidance in the service of proximity." Because attachment behavior has as its aim the maintenance of proximity, the function of this avoidance is to disable feelings and ideas that threaten the real or perceived relationship.

Using the term *betrayal trauma*, Freyd (1996, 2001) explained that forgetting certain kinds of betrayal experiences can be necessary for the individual's adaptation within a traumatic or emotionally damaging environment. Thus, early on, when Sandra was asked to recount her childhood experiences with her parents, she had great difficulty with the task, stating that she "couldn't remember a thing from way back then," a position that was consistent with her general tendency to deactivate attachment. Such instances of inability to recall childhood events are quite common for individuals who are avoidant of attachment (D. Pederson, personal communication, June 2005), with large blocks of time often unaccounted. In a similar vein, when Sandra was questioned about possible experiences of having felt rejected as a child, her terse response was a simple, "No, never," a view she maintained for many months, stating for example, that

3. While George and colleagues found that one of the main distinguishing qualities of the avoidant pattern of attachment is the use of deactivation as a defensive strategy, they also found evidence that avoidant individuals, to some extent, make use of cognitive disconnection, another form of defensive processing described by Bowlby (1980). Cognitive disconnection refers to the process by which responses may become disconnected cognitively from the interpersonal situations that elicited them, leaving the individual unaware of why he is responding the way he is. George and West (2001) found that on the AAP, a measure of attachment that is highly correlated with the AAI, cognitive disconnection is observable when participants develop two story lines that are qualitatively opposite in emotional tone or when there is a high degree of uncertainty or ambivalence expressed in participants' stories. Clinically, I have observed cognitive disconnection, to a certain extent, among avoidant clients as well, sometimes in conjunction with deactivation. Examples include clients who feel and act in opposite directions (e.g., staying in a romantic relationship with someone toward whom little or no emotion is felt); or individuals who express great uncertainty with respect to intimacy, stuck between two partners, unable to form lasting commitments, but then minimizing any feelings of inadequacy that may arise from this difficulty.

her mother would take her shopping "all the time," and that in fact, she had been "spoiled." But, it was a position that was belied later in therapy when I came to understand the extent of her actual hurt and feelings of abandonment whenever her parents would leave for long periods of time.

In one of her more emotional sessions, much later in the treatment, Sandra came in furious at her mother, in tears, for embarrassing her in front of her good friend the evening before. As if it were a humorous anecdote, her mother had openly recollected a story of the time that Sandra, who had been left on her own for the weekend, noticed that the family dog was unable to keep itself balanced and had become ataxic. Alarmed, Sandra lifted the pet into their plastic wagon, taking him to the local veterinarian. The doctor performed an urgent procedure on the animal; Sandra had been given the choice between the expensive operation and putting the pet to sleep as the doctor's office could not reach the parents at their hotel. When they learned what had transpired and the exorbitant cost, her parents accused her of being foolish with money, "sentimental" and "overly sensitive."

As she told me the story at this much later point in the treatment, Sandra was willing to acknowledge her anger at her mother as well as her feelings of abandonment at having to make such a decision on her own, particularly after having lost her nanny a few years earlier during one of her parents' many absences. Her presentation at this later point in therapy now stood in marked contrast to the deactivation that appeared so evident when I had first met her.

### *Minimization of Attachment*

A central aspect of deactivation is the minimization of negative attachment-related experiences. When such events are discussed, the individual minimizes the emotional meaning or long-term implications, often downplaying the negative effects of the experience or its severity (Linehan, 1993). When they come up as a result of clinician questioning, adverse experiences are often glossed over (Alexander et al., 1997; Slade, 1999).

Minimization of attachment can be seen in the responses given on projective tests designed to assess attachment patterns. On the Adult Attachment Projective (AAP), a series of drawings with ambiguous but clearly emotionally charged themes are presented to participants, who are then asked to tell a story from imagination based on what they see in the card (George & West, 2001).

The sixth card, "Ambulance," depicts a child and elderly woman in the foreground, peering at an ambulance just outside their window. A stretcher with a figure in it is being loaded into the ambulance. The implication may be that some important person was removed on a stretcher from the central character's home. In an example given by George and West (2001), after the participant indicated that the parent was taken to the hospital, she stated "everyone acts like normal, as if nothing had happened." Attempts such as this one, to see as "normal" events and situations that are anything but, reflect minimization in action. Alexander (1992) described as "self-deception" the ways in which some formerly abused clients attempt to deal with painful affect, such as the grief accompanying loss or the pain associated with feelings of rejection in the family.

### *Intellectualized Speech or Activity*

Minimization may be found in the form of intellectualized speech or activity. Clients often focus attention on the cognitive elements of experience, such as, say, the legal implications of a family feud or the corresponding financial minutiae, rather than on the emotional aspects of events. Bowlby (1980) viewed this as a form of diversion, noting that at times, intellectual or other time-intensive pursuits may become so consuming that they monopolize the individual's energy, systematically excluding attachment-related experience from being processed. This may come in the form of changing topics toward nonthreatening issues, excessive valuing of work at the expense of romantic relationships, or tremendous time spent on activity-centered friendships.

Approximately 2 months after she initially came to see me for therapy, Sandra became involved with a man from work. Most of her previous relationships had been deeply dissatisfying to her, and she had come to the unhappy conclusion that "when you get right down to it, all men want is sex," and that she would more than likely always be on her own. Initially, she was pleased by how different her current boyfriend was. She had only been in relationships with married men prior to that, her first at the age of 14. Her longest one, an affair she had in high school, also with a married man, ended in her having an abortion and discovering she had contracted a sexually transmitted disease from him.

Not long after Sandra and her current boyfriend became intimate, she began coming in to sessions complaining that he was "always around," that he was "too needy." In time, she became increasingly involved with her book club as well as her rowing team. When I would point out her tendency to screen his calls, sometimes avoiding him for weeks at a time but still not breaking up with him, she would cite differences in their political leanings as an explanation, or she would embark on a detailed listing of the pros and cons of staying with him. Finally, she broke up with him the morning after a weekend trip they had taken together, during which he had confessed to being in love with her. In this way, Sandra would use intellectualization as well as activity-centered pursuits as a way of avoiding her deep-seated fear of closeness and intimacy.

### *Positive Ending*

The minimization of negative attachment-related experiences may be observed in the client's narrative style or storytelling process, most notably by the tendency to put a positive ending, a positive spin on an otherwise deeply distressing story. Main and colleagues described this type of rationalization among speakers being administered the AAI (George et al., 1996; Hesse, 1999), referring to it as "positive wrap-up."

To elaborate on this concept, painful or traumatic experiences cannot be minimized indefinitely or completely. The effects of deactivation are only temporary. Through the course of therapy, individuals in this client population inevitably end up relaying stories that they normally do not share with others, or think about very much, particularly those portraying parents in an unfavorable light. As the therapist asks questions surrounding attachment-related experiences, such as separations, losses, and illnesses, the client may find herself in the process of telling a painful attachment-related story, one that she had never intended to get into or think about when she first walked in the therapist's door. And, a variety of fleeting affective states may surface, including embarrassment, feelings of guilt or shame, anger at the therapist for making her feel vulnerable, and often a sense of being disloyal to a particular parent.

As such a story is being relayed and the client experiences mounting feelings of embarrassment, humiliation, disloyalty, and so on, unbearable feelings need to be managed. Hence, stories emerge that begin one way and end another, as though a happy ending were tacked on in a last-ditch effort to make everything appear fine. In this way, stories of painful experiences may be positively wrapped up, rationalized as in, "It was good for me; it made me strong." Or, a sudden shift occurs in which a parent who was deeply hurtful in one scenario is portrayed glowingly in the next, without any apparent connection between the two scenarios or recognition of the potential inconsistency. Or, as one client explained, after briefly noting the fact that her father had sexually abused her for several years while she was an adolescent, "but he was a very successful and respected judge" in their community. So, she did not think he did what he did "on purpose." When I asked her if she thought his behavior was "an accident," she nodded in a matter-of-fact manner, yes, it was. In such a manner, the client attempts to explain away the deepest of hurts but lacks a coherent explanation regarding what did happen, thus missing out on true resolution.

### *Talking Around*

Another way in which minimization may be observed is in the tendency for such clients to talk around important issues. By discussing and focusing attention on *non*-attachment-related themes, often at great length, there is an avoidance of the more emotionally painful, attachment-related experiences.

Sometimes, it is easy to tell that individuals are ducking important issues. They may focus at length on minor financial worries or assorted disagreements with others, and the avoidance is evident. However, when a client speaks with concern about an issue of obvious importance to him, such as his sexual difficulties, frustrating job, and so on, it may be more difficult to tell that the client is actually using avoidance, particularly when there is an accompanying sense of distress. Nevertheless, it may be that he is minimizing attachment-related experiences in an attempt to deactivate the attachment system, even as he may be feeling upset in a number of other ways.

Drawing on theory, we can see that it is possible for an individual to deactivate attachment, even as he activates other behavioral systems. In discussing the ethological concept of behavioral systems, George and Solomon (1999) noted that the attachment system is but one biologically based system that has evolved to promote survival and reproductive success. Other systems include the caregiving behavioral system, the affiliative system, the sexual system, and the exploratory system. Ethologists maintain that the behavior of humans and other species is organized into these systems. Furthermore, these systems operate in relation to one another, and behavior is a product of their dynamic interaction (Bowlby, 1969/1982; George & Solomon, 1999; Hinde, 1982).

In considering individuals who are avoidant of attachment, it is helpful to keep in mind these different behavioral systems. Doing so allows us to explain why individuals who are avoidant in one domain of experience may appear so very different in another, why, for example, those who avoid attachment may very well be socially active, sexually passionate, or intellectually deep. In other words, deactivation of attachment does not necessarily mean deactivation of the other behavioral systems. In fact, in therapy we often see passionate, socially engaged, or otherwise deep individuals who will go to great lengths to avoid discussing or thinking about their personal, relational lives.

Thus, it is possible for an individual to deactivate attachment, even as he activates other behavioral systems. Taking the issue one step further, we can see that activation of other behavioral systems may actually be used *in order to* deactivate attachment. That is, the individual may make attempts to substitute another behavioral system for attachment. Consider, for example, the client who avoids the development of meaningful intimate relationships by throwing himself into work (exploratory system) over the course of many years. The primary purpose of such diversion is the avoidance of painful attachment-related memories and the feelings arising from the prospect of intimacy, but on the surface, such diversion has the advantage of social acceptability, achievement, and success, all of which tend to eclipse the avoidance.

Interestingly, in activating another behavioral system as a substitute for attachment, there is often a thematic connection to attachment. We often see such a pattern after overwhelming loss, for example, the individual who becomes involved in serial sexual relationships (sexual behavioral system) leading up to and following the death of his spouse by terminal illness in an almost frantic attempt to keep feelings of loss at bay. Or, the young mother who, following the death of her husband, becomes completely consumed by child rearing (caregiving behavioral system), even long after her children have matured into young adults, precluding the possibility of her establishing intimacy and feeling such vulnerability ever again.

Returning now to the concept of talking around attachment-related issues, we can see that it is possible for clients to appear very active in the session, presenting their concerns with distress, discussing matters that are clearly consequential, matters that feel important to them, while concurrently diverting attention away from attachment-related issues. And, that talking around may be used as a means of avoiding issues that are much more difficult for them to manage.

This pattern was apparent in the case of a young man I saw for therapy. In the first session, in which I focused primarily on the current problem, he spent the better part of our time reviewing—in dramatic play-by-play fashion—the details of a recent failed business deal. Although colorful, and at times appearing emotional in the first session, he was like a different person in our next meeting, at which time I interviewed him on his attachment history. The contrast was striking in regard to his level of animation, affect tone, and amount spoken. In this second session, when asked about his early attachments, he responded by shutting down.

I gleaned from him that his was a history of ongoing serial abandonment, in a cycle of promises given and promises broken, severe physical abuse from his father (including a broken nose), alcohol abuse on the part of his mother, and years of mild conduct disorder as a teenager, including a string of minor problems with the law. Nevertheless, his reluctance to discuss these matters openly was evident in terse, controlled responses, many glances at his watch, and a variety of statements that came across as excuses made on his father's behalf, such as "My dad had a lot on his plate," along with unsolicited comments in the form of gratuitous praise (Hesse, 1999), such as "My dad was extremely intelligent, so everyone wanted his opinions." This young man's first session may be characterized as a form of pressured diversion. This is not to say that his feelings around the failed business deal were unimportant, but they were manageable and therefore easier to focus on and talk about than the more painful alternative.

### *Cutting Off*

Having discussed several presentations of the minimization of negative attachment-related experiences, I would like to point out here that, in fact, minimization does not work particularly well. Chapter 2 looks at some of the implications, in terms of psychopathology, of excessive reliance on avoidant defenses, that is, the consequences for mental health that occur when such defenses break down. However, here I note that sometimes attempts to minimize negative attachment experiences fail, and that this seems to occur when the individual is overloaded by attachment-related distress. For example, when hurt or rejection are overwhelmingly strong or when the client is about to come face to face with feelings of profound vulnerability, the minimization strategies described may no longer be adequate to cope, and the individual may turn to stronger measures to deal with painful feelings or memories. Often, she will resort to cutting off the relationship.

We see this frequently in therapy with the client who makes the decision not to talk to her grown child or to a close friend for years on end or at the end of treatment when the individual who had been coming regularly for many months, using therapy actively, seemingly out of the blue stops showing up and fails to return the clinician's messages. For the client who is avoidant of attachment, cutting off the relationship provides temporary relief, a reprieve from having to face feelings that, if expressed, could cause far more damage to the relationship or to the individual's perception of the relationship.

In using the term *cutoff*, I am borrowing from Main (1977), who made use of Chance's (1962) description of cutoff postures, seen in nonhuman species. Such postures included turning away the eyes, turning the head down, and other examples of redirecting attention when in conflict situations. Chance described the adaptive effects that brief avoidance may have in such situations, noting that when an animal is threatened by a member of its own species, a member toward which it is also attracted, cutoff postures enable the threatened animal to remain nearby. Main stressed that the outcome of cutoff was the maintenance of proximity. And as mentioned, Bowlby's (1988) view of attachment avoidance was that it was "in the service of proximity."

Thus, cutting off the relationship, at least for the time being, may paradoxically serve to protect the relationship, or it protects the client from having to face attachment-related distress that has been ignited within that relationship. By deactivating attachment in this way, the client shifts attention away, and no longer has to face the painful conflict, thereby minimizing potential damage.

It is important to add that unlike clients who are preoccupied by their attachment-related experiences (who may also cut off relationships to manage emotional pain), when avoidant clients cut off relationships, they do so in a way that can be remarkably blasé. After all, avoidance is geared toward "cooling down" attachment. Thus, they do not give lengthy reasons for their actions. Instead, little or no explanation may be offered or rationalized reasons may be used, justifications that fail to explain the severity of the actions taken.

As an example, let us return again to the case of Sandra. As a young adult, she went through a period of a few years when she did not talk to her mother. After she had left home at the age of 17, she supported herself while she completed community college. At that point, there were no more children in the house, and her parents went through a contentious divorce that devastated the family financially. Her mother, who had grown up quite religious, but had been away from it throughout Sandra's childhood, returned to the church, pressuring

Sandra to do the same. Her father sank into alcohol abuse and depression, and both her parents would call her to complain bitterly about the other and, on occasion, to borrow money.

Despite the fact that at the point of beginning therapy she had not spoken with her mother for a number of years, and despite the childhood events described in this chapter, when first interviewed on her attachment history, Sandra characterized her mother as having been "loving" and was only able to support this view with examples such as, "She would buy us anything we wanted." In a later session, when I questioned her regarding why she had not spoken with her mother for several years, her response was, "I guess I was—we all get busy, you know? We live in such a busy world."

About a month and a half into treatment, as Sandra became increasingly invested in the therapy process, I pointed out her pattern of cutting relationships out of her life, and that she had done this in a number of contexts. The following interchange took place about halfway through the session.

*Sandra:* It's to eliminate the people who are bringing me down. I like to be friends with people who I can trust. Usually, I'm a very open person. I'll open up to anyone. I'll tell them anything they ask me. Usually with that person, I'll answer any question; it's not like I care. But also people who hurt me, or who just show themselves not to be good people, I tend to cut them. I don't really know why because . . . I'm a very open person [pause, 5 seconds]. Trust is usually not a big concern because [pause] usually it bites me in the ass when I tell people way too much stuff, and then they'll turn it against me. But I always do it, so it's not really something I'm concerned about because I still do it. If it was so bad, I'd stop. But, um [pause, 5 seconds] um . . . what was my point?
*R.M.:* You were talking about eliminating people who were bringing you down.
*Sandra:* Yeah, so, best to eliminate them . . . yeah. . . .

[under her breath] I don't know why [brief pause].

[speaking voice] But that's why it's a good thing, because it's just to get them out, because when they do this, they're not worth it [raises voice at end of sentence, as if asking question].
*R.M.:* Mmm. . . . It's kinda like amputating a part of your body that has been badly damaged, cutting out people who are bringing you down.
*Sandra:* Yeah.
*R.M.:* Yeah.

*Sandra:* Yeah. . . . It's just, you know, if they do something like that, who says they won't do something even worse.
*R.M.:* Uh humm [nods].
*Sandra:* I don't know [pause]. Is it good or bad? I just had to do it. I don't see myself ever going back there and saying sorry for not talking to you, or taking your apologies, or something, or whatever. I'm not a person whose gonna do that. If they're cut, they're cut. And that's how it is. Then I'll usually never see them again.
*R.M.:* I see [nods].

As might be expected, the tendency to cut off relationships became an issue in the therapy, such that Sandra would make periodic attempts to drop treatment, particularly when potential for conflict would emerge between us or when she would appear more vulnerable or reveal less-than-flattering details about herself. In a session that both she and I would come to see as quite meaningful, I asked her to reflect on her pattern of wanting to drop therapy whenever she was in crisis, when it seemed like she "needed me the most." The tendency for individuals in this clinical population to use such *distancing maneuvers*—interactions geared toward creating a comfortable distance between therapist and client in the treatment relationship—is discussed in greater detail in Chapters 5 and 6, in which we get into client and therapist transference and countertransference patterns in the therapeutic interaction.

One final point I would like to make about the cutting off of relationships is that it is sometimes accompanied by inconsistent patterns in parental idealization. As mentioned, when the avoidant client resorts to cutting off relationships, it is because she is having difficulty adequately deactivating attachment-related thoughts and feelings in the usual ways we have been discussing, needing to resort to stronger measures to keep painful feelings at bay. The client's minimization strategies are not working adequately to deal with overwhelmingly strong attachment-related distress, such as profound hurt, rejection, or feelings of vulnerability, so she resorts to cutting off the relationship. At such times, a caregiver, who normally would be discussed in an idealized manner, might be viewed differently. The client may go through a period when she disparages or devalues the parent or raises the other (non-cutoff) parent's status.

Such a situation is confusing for the therapist, who may observe powerful inconsistencies in parental idealization from session to session or even within session. A caregiver who might be described in one instance in idealized terms is now disparaged or devalued. And, the client may show little awareness of the inconsistency or awareness that the parental characterization had been so different previously.

As discussed, cutoff is a paradox. It pushes the relationship away, but in doing so, it serves to protect the relationship, or it protects the client from having to face the attachment-related distress that has been ignited within the relationship. The client engages in cutoff behavior when the direct acknowledgment or expression of feelings is just too frightening. Helping the client articulate ambivalent feelings regarding a parent she may admire but may feel deeply wounded by will be an important aspect of treatment.

### *Self-Perception as Self-Reliant, Independent, Strong, and Normal*

Patterns of attachment develop in the context of experiences with caregivers, experiences through which children develop expectations about how future interactions will operate (Bretherton, 1990; Main et al. 1985). In Bowlby's view, over time, children come to internalize their experiences such that the parent's responses to the child's signals have a strong impact on whether the child is put on a path for secure or insecure development (Muller, Kraftcheck, & McLewin, 2004).

In considering these internalized expectations, Bowlby distinguished between internal working models of the *self* and internal working models of *other people.* The former refers to "whether or not the self is judged to be the sort of person towards whom anyone, and the attachment figure in particular, is likely to respond in a helpful way," while the latter refers to "whether or not the attachment figure is judged to be the sort of person who in general responds to calls for support and protection" (1973, p. 204). These internalized expectations are particularly important in the context of treatment as psychotherapy, to a large extent, is about helping modify problematic expectations people have developed regarding their interpersonal world. Bartholomew and colleagues have paid especially close attention to the aspect of Bowlby's theory focusing on working models of self and other in the development of their approach to adult attachment (Bartholomew & Horowitz, 1991; Bartholomew & Shaver, 1998).

How are internal working models of self and other relevant to the avoidant client? Individuals who deactivate attachment miss out on important information and therefore miss out on growth opportunities in the relational world. As the individual develops, the tendency to deactivate and devalue attachment experiences, to use minimization in the various forms described, yields a worldview of others as unreliable. And, if others cannot be relied on, the tendency is to fall back on the self (George & West, 2001). The counterdependence (Bartholomew & Horowitz, 1991) seen in such clients comes from a necessity to compensate for a fundamental failure to believe in the availability of important others.

As attachment continues to be avoided over the course of the life span, experiences accumulate that serve to strengthen this way of seeing things, and fail to disconfirm it. If one constructs a world that lacks interdependence, opportunities for intimacy become fewer and farther between over time. When reliance on others is viewed as a sign of fundamental weakness, dependence must be avoided. Sadly, the very word *avoid* tells us what is left behind by a relentless pattern of falling back on the self: *a void.* That is, a sense of inner emptiness, an internalized view that, in times of need, others simply cannot be called on for support or protection.

Thus, there is a tendency for avoidant clients to consciously perceive and present themselves as self-reliant, independent, strong, and normal (Bartholomew & Horowitz, 1991; Eagle, 1996). If attachment-related distress needs to be resolved, they find it exceedingly difficult to turn to others for help. Turning back to the case of Sandra, it is interesting that in one of our earlier sessions, when I asked about her adolescent years, she told me that she had been living on her own since she was 17, and that one of the few things she remembered about her childhood was realizing at a young age that if you needed anyone, the only person you could truly count on was yourself.

In a poignant example using the AAP (George & West, 2001), a measure in which stimulus cards are designed to activate the participant's attachment system, the authors described an individual's response to the final card, "Child in Corner." The card depicts a child standing in the corner with arms up (as if possibly responding to some threat), head turned away. The card activates the attachment system around themes of perceived threat or danger, often pulling for stories of child punishment or maltreatment. In an example given by the authors on the extensive use of self-reliance among individuals avoidant of attachment, the participant tells a story of physical punishment, describing the protagonist, a boy, as putting his hands up as an act of resistance, coping with the situation through his "capacity to act" (George & West, 2001), but at no point turning to attachment figures or to other important relationships for help, instead trying to manage the frightening circumstances alone.

This example is consistent with the results of several studies in experimental social psychology. In a series of well-designed empirical investigations of adults in highly stressful or threatening circumstances (e.g., military training, being reminded of one's mortality, etc.), psychologist Mario Mikulincer and colleagues found that to deal with distressing stimuli, adults who were avoidant of attachment tended not to engage in support seeking as a coping strategy, instead falling back on "distancing" strategies, distancing themselves from significant others to manage their distress (e.g., Mikulincer & Florian, 1995, 2000).

The term *compulsive self-reliance* was borrowed by Bowlby (1980) from Parkes (1973), whose studies on persistent phantom pain in amputees demonstrated greater risk for psychophysiological sequelae following surgery among individuals who had such beliefs as, "There are two kinds of people in this world, the weak and the strong," and "Always be on your guard with people." In discussing self-reliance, Bowlby drew on a series of case studies conducted by psychoanalyst Helene Deutsch (1937), who described what appeared to be a striking absence of grief or mourning among some individuals following important experiences of loss. Commenting on her cases, Bowlby (1980) stressed that beneath the hard shell of proclaimed self-sufficiency lies a strong wish to be loved and cared for. Preferring the term *insistent self-reliance*, Sable (2000) noted the lack of confidence some clients experience in the availability of attachment figures, going on to say that they avoid and deny the need for support and attention, defensively proclaiming a self-sufficiency that hides their fear of trusting others.

Self-reliance, then, fills a gap that arises in a world in which attachment is devalued, and the individual cannot count on close relationships. Hand in hand with self-reliance goes a self-perception of competence. Self-reliance is not quite enough if a sense of competence is lacking. Thus, there is also a self-imposed pressure on those avoidant of attachment to perceive themselves as normal and strong, whether that is true or not. On the AAI (George et al., 1996; Hesse, 1999), there is a tendency among such clients to "normalize;" for the individual to describe herself as having experienced a childhood that was normal, typical, or okay.

Similarly, such individuals will present themselves as "strong" when explaining why they rarely cry or why they think they can handle this or that problem. In attempting to emphasize strength, they often convey themes that place weight on personal achievement (George & West, 2001) as well as material success, such as wealth, degrees, and professional designations.

Finally, related to the self-perceptions discussed, there is a tendency for avoidant clients to seek psychotherapy primarily for symptom-based reasons. The difficulty they experience in asking for help or in acknowledging the need for help (Dozier & Bates, 2004; Shorey & Snyder, 2006) puts them in the position of holding off on therapy until they are symptomatic or until there are substantial problems to address. The self-perception of both independence and normality makes it difficult to acknowledge the need for help.

It is important to note that these self-perceptions (self-reliant, independent, strong, and normal) are all relatively inflated and brittle. They are consciously perceived attributes that avoidant clients ascribe to themselves in a compensatory manner; fragile self-perceptions that are prone to break down when the individual becomes symptomatic (detailed in Chapter 2). In treatment, there is an opportunity to reexamine these self-perceptions, their development, and the helpful and unhelpful effects they have had on the person's life.

## Avoidance, Trauma, and What Research Tells Us

To this point, we have focused on the nature of avoidant defenses and have looked at some examples of clients with histories of intrafamilial or attachment-based trauma who demonstrate this kind of defensive processing. There are two research-related questions that some readers may be asking themselves, each of which I address here.

First, when we consider clients with such trauma histories, just how often do we actually see the avoidant pattern of attachment? Is this a common enough problem that we should be concerned? A few studies have addressed this question. Research that we conducted (e.g., Muller, Lemieux, & Sicoli, 2001; Muller, Sicoli, & Lemieux, 2000), looking at 66 high-risk adults with histories of childhood abuse, estimated the dismissing-avoidant pattern at about 42%. The same figure was reported in a study by Levy and colleagues (2006), who treated 90 adults diagnosed with borderline personality disorder (a diagnosis known to be associated with high levels of intrafamilial trauma). At the start of treatment, 42% were assigned to the primary AAI category of dismissing-avoidant.

Both higher and lower figures have been reported as well. On the higher end, Weinfield, Sroufe, and Egeland (2000) found that 60% of individuals in a sample of high-risk young adults were classified on the AAI as dismissing-avoidant. More modest figures were reported in research by Stovall-McClough and Cloitre (2006) and Allen and colleagues (2001). The former classified between 10% and 23% (of traumatized adults) as dismissing-avoidant, while the latter reported between 17% and 19%. Finally, meta-analytic studies by van IJzendoorn and Bakermans-Kranenburg estimated levels of dismissing-avoidant attachment at 32% for the violence-within-family category and at 20% and 36% among subjects grouped into post-traumatic and abusive, respectively (groups associated with high levels of intrafamilial trauma) (Bakermans-Kranenburg & van IJzendoorn, 2009; van IJzendoorn & Bakermans-Kranenburg, 2008).

Given the research conducted to date, a reasonable estimate would consider about 30% of adult survivors of intrafamilial trauma to be avoidant of attachment. However, A. F. Lieberman (2004) emphasized the need for more research systematically documenting the extent to which direct exposure may be linked to specific attachment-related outcomes.

A second important research-related question may be considered here as well: What do studies on working with this particular clinical population tell us? In considering specific interventions with trauma survivors who are avoidant of attachment, we need to examine prior clinical and research studies regarding treatment outcome and process. Unfortunately, the literature on treatment outcome is highly limited for this population, and when we look at treatment specifics, the literature is sparser still.

The few clinical papers addressing the topic examined the role of attachment patterns, in general, in the psychotherapy of trauma survivors (Sable, 2000; Slade, 2004) and included populations such as individuals with histories of incest (Alexander & Anderson, 1994) and clients with complex trauma (Pearlman & Courtois, 2005). However, these articles have tended to focus more on broad differences in the way that treatment unfolds among clients with different attachment patterns. Thus, the emphasis in these prior papers has been less specific in regard to particular recommendations for intervention.

The few empirical studies conducted to date have found trauma survivors with the avoidant attachment pattern to be especially challenging, particularly in regard to the therapeutic relationship, showing more difficulties in the therapeutic alliance toward the end of treatment (e.g., Kanninen, Salo, & Punamaki, 2000) and showing greater likelihood of relapse in terms of attachment insecurity during the post-treatment period (Muller & Rosenkranz, 2009; Rosenkranz, Muller, & Bedi, 2007). Some studies (e.g., Tasca, Balfour, Ritchie, & Bissada, 2007) have looked at other high-risk groups (i.e., those with eating disorders) and, similar to Kanninen et al. (2000), have found weaker therapeutic alliances among clients who were avoidant of attachment (Tasca et al., 2007). Interestingly, in a randomized controlled trial of transference-focused psychotherapy for high-risk clients with borderline personality disorder, a diagnosis known to be associated with high rates of intrafamilial abuse, the authors reported significant improvements from insecure to secure attachment, regardless of attachment pattern at outset (Levy et al., 2006). And, in contrast to some of the findings discussed, a well-known study by Fonagy and colleagues (1996) examined longer-term individual and group psychoanalytic psychotherapy, also on clients diagnosed with borderline personality disorder. In that study, the authors found that improvements in global assessment of functioning scores were, in fact, stronger for those avoidant of attachment than they were for clients with other insecure attachment patterns at the start of treatment.

Unfortunately, the empirical studies summarized have all tended to focus, in relatively general terms, on the ways in which different attachment patterns are associated with overall symptom change. Elsewhere (e.g., Muller, 2009), I have noted that theory and research on specific intervention strategies for this clinical population have been lacking. (In articles by Gormley [2004] and Davila and Levy [2006], similar arguments have been advanced regarding the application of attachment theory to clinical practice.) The emphasis in many of the prior clinical articles and empirical investigations on this population has not been so much on "what we can *do* to help" as on "why these clients are so *hard* to help," which, unfortunately, is of limited practical use in the consulting room. The majority of this book (from Chapter 3 on) is therefore devoted to looking at specific intervention strategies with this clinical population; some I have described elsewhere (e.g., Muller, 2006, 2007, 2009; Muller, Bedi, Zorzella, & Classen, 2008). After all, theory and research on any client group is useful to the extent that it can inform clinical practice.

## Clarifications Regarding "Avoidance" in the Current Context

There are a couple of final points that should be made regarding the word *avoidance* and its use here. The term itself has different meanings within the psychological literature, among various practitioners, and across different treatment modalities. For example, readers coming to this book with a strong background in attachment theory will read the term very differently from those coming with more traditional training in mental health diagnosis. There are two important points that may be made regarding this issue. First is the matter of terminology and labeling. In the theoretical and research literatures, a number of terms have been used for avoidant attachment, depending on whether the author was writing for a developmental psychiatry, clinical, or social-personality readership. These include, among others, the terms: *dismissing*, *avoidant*, and *dismissing-avoidant*. For the sake of simplicity and consistency in the current context, these are all referred to as *avoidant attachment* throughout the majority of this book.

Second, avoidant attachment *is not the same* as avoidant personality disorder. Individuals coming from outside the area of attachment theory may find this a bit more confusing. However, avoidant personality disorder, as defined in the fourth edition, text revision, of the Diagnostic and Statistical Manual of Mental Disorders (DSM-IV-TR; American Psychiatric Association, 2000), is a pervasive pattern of social inhibition, feelings of inadequacy, and hypersensitivity by which the client demonstrates the avoidance of work or school activities, risk aversion, fear of being embarrassed, and other features of social avoidance. While a number of individuals who are avoidant of attachment may also demonstrate features of avoidant personality disorder, these two domains are clearly distinct and should be treated as such. Thus, for the reader who is more accustomed to the *DSM* use of "avoidance," it is important to keep in mind that what we are discussing in this book is the *avoidance of attachment* specifically, and all that goes along with it, much of which has been described in this chapter.

## Summing Up

What do clients such as Sandra teach us about avoidant defenses? As discussed in the chapter, early in our work, she tended to rely heavily on deactivation as a strategy to cope with attachment-related distress. Shifting attention away from events or feelings that would arouse her attachment system, she avoided painful emotions and evaded memories of traumatic relationship experiences with her parents. Engaging in parental idealization, she would turn her attention away from information that threatened a positive image of her early attachment relationships. Her tendency to minimize the emotional meaning of traumatic events and their long-term implications was apparent in the way she glossed over such experiences, detached herself from emotional expression when traumatic events surfaced, or viewed dwelling on such experiences as unnecessary.

When stories indicative of trauma arose, Sandra would put positive endings on them, rationalizing away painful feelings or hurts. She would also talk around them, focusing on issues that she experienced as important but that diverted attention away from themes of vulnerability. Further, as a way of avoiding uncomfortable attachment-related emotions, she would rely heavily on intellectualized thinking and activity. Reluctant to turn to others in times of need, Sandra tended to fall back on herself. A deeply self-reliant person, she took a view of herself as independent, strong, and normal, making it difficult for her to acknowledge the fact that she needed and wanted help when she first came to see me for treatment.

When the expression of certain emotions felt unmanageable in important relationships, she cut off the relationships, at least for a time. This tendency became a theme in the therapy. When there was some danger that she might rely on me too much or express attachment-related emotions, such as sadness, rejection, disappointment, or anger toward me, she made attempts to distance herself in a number of ways, a tendency that I brought to her attention and that became instructive throughout our work together.

CHAPTER 2

# Activating the Attachment System and Challenging the Client

Chapter 1 discussed the nature of avoidant defenses, such as the use of deactivation as a defense against traumatic distress. Having reviewed such concepts as minimization, idealization, and self-reliance, we now begin to consider what theory and research suggests in regard to intervention. We look at an argument in favor of actively turning attention toward painful attachment-related experiences and challenging defensive avoidance.

Let us examine why such an approach makes sense with this population, why it is important, and why it is not so easy to implement in practice.

## Empirical Support for an Approach That Activates the Attachment System

As mentioned in Chapter 1, many difficulties have been documented for clients who tend to use defensive avoidance, and these difficulties have been detailed in the research literature (e.g., Berant, Mikulincer, & Florian, 2001; Edelstein, 2007; Edelstein & Gillath, 2008; Edelstein & Shaver, 2004). Empirical studies have pointed to a host of psychological problems, including negative health- and mental-health-related consequences. In particular, research indicates that avoidant defenses require enormous effort to sustain and are not particularly robust because they are prone to break down in the face of high stress in general and attachment-related distress in particular.

The intervention strategies presented throughout this book are guided, in part, by an approach that addresses the defensive patterns favored by such clients. That is, a treatment approach that activates the attachment system,[1] one that turns attention toward attachment-related experiences and challenges defensive avoidance. Without such challenge, the therapist runs the risk of colluding with avoidant coping patterns that may evade distress in the short run yet turn out to be ineffective over time (Bernier & Dozier, 2002; Dozier & Bates, 2004).

There are three bodies of psychological research that point to a general treatment approach that favors activating the attachment system and challenging avoidant defenses. These are presented next.

### *Unless Deactivation Is Challenged, the Client Will Not Change*

Individuals who are avoidant of attachment put considerable psychological effort into closing off discussion of threatening issues. Unless challenged, such issues will likely remain closed off.

Deactivation, as discussed in Chapter 1, is a central defensive characteristic of avoidant attachment. It has as its goal to shift the individual's attention away from those feelings, situations, or memories that arouse the attachment system. It enables the person to diminish, minimize, or devalue the importance of attachment-related stimuli (George & West, 2001). Experimental studies by researchers Shaver, Mikulincer, and Edelstein (e.g., Edelstein, 2007; Edelstein & Gillath, 2008; Edelstein & Shaver, 2004; Mikulincer, Dolev, & Shaver, 2004), looking at attentional biases, have supported the hypothesis that avoidant individuals turn their attention away from attachment-related material. Importantly, these researchers found that the avoidant participant's tendency to direct attention away from attachment-related stimuli breaks down when under

1. Activation of the attachment system as an important element of the psychotherapy process was discussed in an article by Liotti (2007).

increased "cognitive load," demonstrating that deactivation of attachment is a mentally effortful process. That is, avoidant persons turn attention away from issues that activate the attachment system, and such active suppression requires considerable mental effort.

Similar findings have been reported by Dozier and her colleagues (e.g., Dozier & Kobak, 1992), who questioned participants about their attachment-related experiences using the Adult Attachment Interview (AAI; George et al., 1996). They found that, among the avoidant interviewees, there were greater rises in skin conductance, indicating higher levels of anxiety, when discussing attachment-related experiences, despite the fact that they consciously denied feeling distress. Dozier's findings further corroborate the notion that, for such individuals, the suppression of attachment-related material is a mentally taxing process. In other words, what these experimental studies showed is that avoidance requires considerable effort. Those who are avoidant of attachment work very hard (psychologically speaking) to keep attachment-related issues out of awareness.

Turning to individual psychotherapy, we see that in treatment, attachment-related material is often closed off from discussion (George & West, 2004). What the research just discussed tells us is that defensive avoidance is *not* easy. It takes a lot of effort to keep attachment-related issues closed off from discussion. Unless challenged, such issues will likely remain closed off, or as is often the case with brighter, analytic individuals, the underlying emotional meaning will remain closed off (Slade, 1999), rendering it impossible to engage in true self-examination in psychotherapy.

In discussing the ways in which attachment theory can help inform clinical practice, Bowlby (1988) stated:

> A therapist applying attachment theory sees his role as being one of providing the conditions in which his patient can explore his representational models of himself and his attachment figures with a view to reappraising and restructuring them in the light of the new understanding he acquires and the new experiences he has in the therapeutic relationship. (p. 138)

Bowlby (1988) went on to state that the clinician hopes to "enable his patient to cease being slave to old and unconscious stereotypes and to feel, to think, and to act in new ways" (p. 139). Similarly, psychiatrist David Scharff referred to the field of psychotherapy as the "growth and development business" (Labriola, Carlson, & Kjos, 1998).

In treatment, the continued avoidance of painful attachment-related experiences and events precludes the possibility of helping the client rework problematic models of self and other, and failing to rework representational models of self and other renders the enterprise of psychotherapy less meaningful and long lasting, the unfortunate consequence being an indefinite circling around difficult topics without addressing them substantively. When clients describe psychotherapy as an opportunity "to vent," something important may be missing from the process.

In discussing avoidant attachment patterns in psychotherapy, Holmes (1997) indicated that as a result of such circling around, therapy sessions may seem vacuous and difficult to recall when writing up notes. In a similar vein, Wallin (2007) referred to the avoidant pattern of attachment as a closed system, and that having learned not to acknowledge or express attachment-related distress, such clients struggle in treatment unless they are met with a more active therapeutic stance.

Researchers in the area of short-term dynamic psychotherapy (e.g., McCullough and colleagues) have referred to "affect phobias" as the fear and avoidance of one's own emotional responses, such as anxiety, guilt, shame, or fear of rejection (McCullough, 1998, 2001; McCullough & Andrews, 2001). Thus, a number of investigators (e.g., Schore, 2008) have argued in favor of focusing psychotherapy more intensively on affective experiences, with some (e.g., Connors, 1997; Meyer & Pilkonis, 2001) suggesting that treatment of avoidant clients in particular include strategies that facilitate emotional engagement. Interestingly, studies have demonstrated that the greater the ratio of affect to defenses expressed in session, the greater the improvement observed at outcome (McCullough et al., 2001; Taurke, McCullough, Winston, Pollack, & Flegenheimer, 1990). In addition, neurocognitive investigations (e.g., M. D. Lieberman et al., 2007) have begun to lend support to the long-held notion that *affect labeling* (putting feelings into words) can play a significant role in managing negative emotional experiences.[2]

2. Neuroimaging studies have begun to suggest a possible neurocognitive pathway for the process by which affect labeling (putting feelings into words) can help manage negative emotional experiences. A functional magnetic resonance imaging study by M. D. Lieberman et al. (2007) indicated that affect labeling, in comparison to other forms of encoding, diminished the response

With clients who have histories of intrafamilial trauma, we inevitably come across such painful questions as, "If my mother were indeed so loving, why didn't she protect me from the abuse?" These are questions that have no clear answers but need to be asked nonetheless. As detailed in Chapter 3, there is often anxiety on the part of therapists in hearing and fully addressing painful trauma-related stories. Researchers Cohen, Mannarino, and colleagues have stressed the need for clinicians to become comfortable with listening to such material and with examining the impact of such experiences on the client's life, noting that even subtle reluctance on the therapist's part is communicated in the interaction, and that the individual often withholds telling the full story out of fear that the therapist might not be able to tolerate it (Cohen, Mannarino, & Deblinger, 2006; A. Mannarino, personal communication, October 2005).

Consequently, Dozier and colleagues (Bernier & Dozier, 2002; Dozier & Tyrrell, 1998) cautioned against the therapist's first natural inclination to respond to the avoidance of painful attachment-related topics by "respectfully going along, engaging on superficial, nonthreatening issues" (Bernier & Dozier, 2002, p. 38). Instead, they encouraged a therapeutic stance that "gently challenges" the client's defensive strategies. Similarly, Dozier and Bates warned of the therapist inadvertently providing confirmatory evidence of the avoidant individual's worldview. The authors underlined the importance of psychotherapy being oriented toward helping the client "change expectations" (2004, p. 173).

### *Therapist–Client Dyads With Contrasting Attachment Styles Tend to Work Better*

A second body of research, also pointing to a treatment approach that favors activating the attachment system, has arisen from the issue of the client–therapist match in treatment. That is, individuals who are avoidant of attachment appear to do better when paired with clinicians who have a tendency to be much more activating and who challenge their usual relational stance.

Research has begun to explore the match between client and therapist attach-

---

of the amygdala and other limbic regions to negative emotional images. More specifically, the results suggested that affect labeling may diminish emotional reactivity along a pathway from the right ventrolateral prefrontal cortex (RVLPFC) to the medial prefrontal cortex (MPFC) to the amygdala (M. D. Lieberman et al., 2007).

ment patterns. While only a handful of studies have directly addressed this matter, some initial patterns are beginning to emerge. Increasingly, such studies have been demonstrating stronger effects when clients and therapists relate to one another in a way that is *noncomplementary*, or contrasting of client expectations (Dozier & Tyrrell, 1998). Studies evaluating adult attachment patterns in therapist–client dyads are beginning to show that therapists and clients with dissimilar attachment tendencies have a greater likelihood for treatment success. Bernier and Dozier (2002) indicated that in such dyads, the dissimilar attachment style of the therapist makes it more likely that she will take on a stance that runs counter to what the client pulls for, consequently disconfirming client expectations and perceptions.

In one study, Bernier and colleagues administered the AAI to counseling dyads in an academic setting. They found support for the noncomplementary hypothesis, using both objective and subjective measures of outcome, such that for students who were avoidant of attachment, the most effective matches were with counselors who valued relationships, connectedness, and interdependence (Bernier & Dozier, 2002). In a similar study, Tyrrell, Dozier, Teague, and Fallot (1999) found that for psychiatric patients and their case managers—all of whom had been administered the AAI—better results were reported for the noncomplementary dyads. Of relevance here, patients considered to be avoidant worked significantly better and demonstrated better outcomes when paired with clinicians who were more activating of attachment.

It is important to note that among the few investigations to date on attachment patterns in treatment dyads, none has been conducted specifically on clients with significant histories of intrafamilial trauma. The Tyrrell et al. (1999) study did look at patients with serious psychiatric disorders, many of whom were diagnosed with varying degrees of depression and comorbid substance abuse disorder. But as noted by Bernier and Dozier (2002), considerably more research is needed on the role that noncomplementarity of attachment plays among client and therapist in psychotherapy.

What is also unclear at this point is the full range of factors that may give some therapists the capacity to adjust their style of attachment-activation depending on the particular needs of the client. Mallinckrodt and colleagues described this process as the therapist systematically regulating the level of emotional distance in the relationship to create a corrective emotional experience relative to the client's attachment pattern (Mallinckrodt, 2000; Mallinckrodt, Porter, & Kivlighan, 2005). Some theorists (e.g., Dozier & Bates, 2004) have suggested that securely attached clinicians are likely in the best position to make such adjustments. Indeed, Dozier, Cue, and Barnett (1994) found that secure clinicians demonstrated the greatest flexibility and were the most likely to adjust their style of intervention to provide noncomplementary responses to clients. This ability to regulate emotional distance in the relationship may be, in part, what allows securely attached clinicians to be in the best position to negotiate significant challenges to the therapy, such as ruptures within the therapeutic relationship (Meyer & Pilkonis, 2001).

Despite limitations, the research conducted to date does initially suggest that for clients who are inclined to defend against attachment-related distress through the use of avoidance, improved likelihood for successful outcome may be found with a therapist who is more likely to activate the individual's attachment system and to present a challenge to the client's usual experience of relationships. This notion is consistent with Bowlby's (1988) view that a therapist applying attachment theory provides an environment within which the individual can learn to feel, to think, and to act in new ways within the interpersonal world.

### *Deactivation Turns Out to Be a Poor Means of Coping*

A final body of research that points toward activating attachment and challenging defensive avoidance comes from the examination of defensive breakdown. Specifically, the defensive strategy of deactivation, favored by clients who are avoidant of attachment, is prone to break down under high stress and is associated with significant health- and mental-health-related costs. Consequently, helping individuals build healthier patterns of coping and relating may yield tangible, meaningful benefits.

Researchers examining the development of psychopathology across the life span have found that the defenses used by avoidant individuals become ineffective when the person is under high levels of situational stress, particularly stress that is attachment related. That is, deactivation may work adequately as a defense when psychological demands are minimal. However, in more demanding contexts, such as attachment-related stressful life events (e.g., life-threatening illness, birth of a child, divorce), avoidant defenses become incapacitated and tend to break down (Edelstein & Shaver, 2004; Mikulincer & Shaver, 2003).

Evidence that avoidant defenses dissolve under conditions of attachment-related distress can be found in the experimental and naturalistic investigations of Mikulincer and colleagues (e.g., Mikulincer et al., 2004; Mikulincer & Florian, 1998; Mikulincer & Shaver, 2003). In one particularly compelling study by Mikulincer and Florian (1998), the authors showed that deactivating coping patterns (e.g., ignoring, distancing, not seeking social support) were linked to subsequent psychosomatic symptoms attributable to stress in survivors of Scud missile attacks. Similar findings have emerged in studies of maternal reactions to the birth of a child with congenital heart disease (Berant et al., 2001) and in clinical case studies (Sable, 2000). Interestingly, some of the Mikulincer studies (e.g., Mikulincer et al., 2004) have even shown that once avoidant defenses begin to break down, characteristics of poor underlying self-image begin to emerge, that is, negative views of self that are usually masked by defensiveness. The positive self-image that avoidant individuals normally claim to have is therefore fragile (Shorey & Snyder, 2006) and "appears to lack balance, integration, and inner coherence" (Mikulincer, 1995, p. 1212).

Consistent with findings on defensive breakdown under conditions of high stress, a number of researchers have found negative consequences for well-being over time (Shedler, Mayman, & Manis, 1993). Empirical studies in developmental psychopathology and health psychology have demonstrated associations between higher levels of avoidance and subsequent increases in depression (Edelstein & Gillath, 2008) as well as associations between emotional suppression and risk for the development of cardiovascular disease (Mauss & Gross, 2004) and elevations in blood pressure (Jorgensen, Johnson, Kolodziej, & Schreer, 1996). Research by Edelstein (2007) demonstrated that among avoidant individuals, active inhibition of attachment-related material is predictive of increased psychopathology over time, suggesting that the use of defensive avoidance has long-term psychological costs.

Clinicians working in therapy with children who have been abused or neglected have made similar arguments. For example, Eliana Gil (2006) indicated that although suppression of trauma-related material may provide temporary relief, it requires sustained efforts to maintain, will not allow for the understanding required to achieve normative functioning, and will collapse over time.

In a detailed review, Shedler et al. (1993) concluded that the process of inhibiting thoughts and feelings entails physiological work, reflected in the short run in autonomic reactivity and in the long run in increased health problems. Interestingly, the results of empirical research are highly consistent with the position advanced by Bowlby (1980) in his analysis of defensive exclusion and the extent to which it is associated with behavior that is biologically adaptive. Bowlby considered it to be, ultimately, a handicap in dealings with others, leading to ineffective coping with the interpersonal environment and to breakdowns in functioning over time.

In summary, prior research points to significant health and mental health-related consequences associated with defensive avoidance and indicates that the defensive process of deactivation is highly effortful and prone to break down in the face of high stress in general and attachment-related distress in particular. Prior research is also suggestive of a general treatment approach that runs counter to the defensive strategy favored by such individuals, namely, an approach that is challenging of defensive avoidance and therefore disconfirming of client expectations and perceptions.

## Why Activating Attachment and Challenging Defensive Avoidance Is Not So Easy

As described, the development of specific intervention strategies for this clinical population has been slow. Although there is much written about the frustrations of working with such clients, there is far less that can be used to guide treatment. In part, this may be because avoidance *is* so hard to address. Activating attachment and challenging defensive avoidance is not so straightforward. For one thing, individuals who have histories of trauma, but who use defensive avoidance, present a powerful paradox early in the treatment process, making intervention complicated. They are ambivalent about engaging in therapy, so they pull the therapist in opposing directions, making it hard to work with them.

### *The Treatment Paradox*

When coming for psychotherapy, individuals with histories of intrafamilial trauma are often polysymptomatic. Intrafamilial trauma is now known to be associated with a host of psychological factors and mental health challenges that place the individual at risk for the development of psychopathology across the life span (Briere, 1988; Muller et al., 2004; Stovall-McClough & Cloitre, 2006). Yet, those who are avoidant of attachment also demonstrate the tendency to be highly help rejecting, defensive, and minimizing. Horowitz (1976, 2001) described the appearance of denial and general emotional numbness that follow traumatic events for many such clients. Despite a psychological vulnerability that arises from a history of trauma, these individuals put forth significant defensive efforts to maintain a view of self as strong, independent, self-reliant, and normal.

These opposing factors converge to put the client—and therefore, the therapist as well—into a dilemma: Considering and talking about traumatic events flies in the face of defensive avoidance. Yet, failing to recognize one's history flies in the face of reality.

In treatment, when the therapist makes empathic statements recognizing how difficult or painful a particular experience must have been, the comment is quickly dismissed with brittle, cavalier denial (Wallin pointed out that such individuals often experience empathic statements as "lame substitutes for 'real' help"; 2007, p. 213). Yet, when the clinician is pulled in the direction of keeping things light, she becomes complicit in the act of minimizing traumatic events, failing to provide the client with a psychologically safe environment within which to explore painful life experiences.

In her seminal work, *Trauma and Recovery*, Judith Herman (1992) described the "central dialectic of psychological trauma" as the conflict between the will to deny traumatic events and the will to proclaim them aloud. She explained that while there is a strong will to bury atrocities, denial is but a temporary solution; ghosts surface eventually. She viewed the process of remembering and truth-telling to be critical to the healing process. However, much of the time, the desire to bury the truth, to cope with events through a climate of secrecy—indeed to be coerced into secrecy by those in positions of authority—means that truths tend to surface not as clear verbal narratives but as symptoms.

Both clinical wisdom and prior empirical research (e.g., Alexander, 1992) on the effects of intrafamilial trauma point to the detrimental effects of sweeping traumatic events under the rug. Previous trauma theorists have described the countertransference that emerges with such individuals as the tendency to engage in a "mutual avoidance" (Alexander & Anderson, 1994) that provides relief for both therapist and client (Davies & Frawley, 1994). However, to minimize the importance of such experiences is to be complicit in the act often committed by the parent bystander, that is, replication of the failure to protect. In so doing, the therapist fails to provide a context for the exploration of painful life events. Furthermore, failing to help clients face their traumatic experiences also means colluding in a game of pretend. And psychotherapy, without honesty, amounts to very little.

In describing the fundamental premise of the psychotherapeutic work as a belief in the "restorative power of truth-telling," Herman (1992) wrote:

> From the outset, the therapist should place great emphasis on the importance of truth-telling and full disclosure, since the patient is likely to have many secrets, including secrets from herself. The therapist should make clear that the truth is a goal constantly to be striven for, and that while difficult to achieve at first, it will be attained more fully in the course of time. (pp. 148, 181)

### *Grounding Treatment in a Secure Therapeutic Relationship*

So far in this chapter, we have considered a general treatment approach that favors activating attachment and challenging defensive avoidance. As described, unless such challenges occur, the clinician runs the risk of colluding with defensive coping patterns that may avoid emotional distress for a short while but in time will turn out to be detrimental for the individual. We have reviewed research on the topic, most of which lends support to this approach. However, we have noted that activating attachment and challenging defensive avoidance is not so straightforward. Clients who have histories of trauma, but who use defensive avoidance, present a powerful paradox early in the process. As stated, they are ambivalent about engaging in treatment and therefore pull the therapist in opposing directions, making it complicated to work with them.

There are other reasons why challenging defensive avoidance can be difficult. For the therapist who places a high premium on the importance of the therapeutic relationship, a more activating, challenging approach can present a variety of problems. In my experience, most therapists working with trauma survivors value the therapeutic relationship, namely, the establishment of security, safety, and a climate of empathy; so understanding how to balance the "secure base" of the therapeutic relationship against the complexities inherent in challenging defensive avoidance reflects both skill and artfulness in the therapy. Let us here consider the importance of the therapeutic relationship in the treatment of trauma and then the complications to the relationship that arise out of a more activating therapeutic stance.

With clients who have experienced suffering at the hands of the important people in their lives, the centrality of the therapeutic relationship to the healing process cannot be emphasized enough.[3,4] Liotti (2004), who has written extensively on attachment and the psychotherapeutic relationship, explained that when clinicians are developing treatment priorities in their work with clients who have trauma histories, striving for safety and alliance within the therapeutic relationship should take precedence. In a similar vein, Pearlman and Courtois (2005) emphasized the importance of the therapeutic relationship with such high-risk clients, explaining that the relationship should be marked by respect, information, connection, and hope. In their approach to treatment, the development of a secure therapeutic relationship gives rise to opportunities to examine views of self and other and to build interpersonal and self-regulation skills.

Other attachment theorists have espoused similar approaches to intervention. Drawing on Bowlby's (1988) concept of the secure base in treatment, Jeremy Holmes (2001) discussed the critical importance of responsiveness and empathic attunement in the psychotherapeutic relationship:

> A secure base arises out of the responsiveness and attunement provided by the therapist. Attunement is, by its very nature, non-controlling, following rather than leading, affective rather than instrumental. It is "aimless" in the sense that it cannot legislate in advance for what will emerge from the playful and spontaneous encounter between therapist and patient . . . You cannot prescribe what is going to happen in a ses-

3. Summarizing the results of both his and others' studies on the neurobiology of attachment and human development, Schore (2008) discussed implications for treatment and indicated that "more than insight, interactive regulation within the *therapeutic alliance* is a central mechanism in the treatment of patients with a history of early relational trauma" (emphasis added).

4. Comprehensive meta-analytic studies (e.g., Wampold, 2001), which summarize findings across many investigations and different treatment models, have found the relationship between therapist and client to be a critical factor in successful outcome in psychotherapy.

> sion . . . What *can* be prescribed are the conditions favorable to secure base. (p. 50)

In my own work, and throughout my training, the treatment relationship has always been of central importance. Concepts such as clinician responsiveness, attunement, empathy, and genuineness in the therapeutic interaction are all fundamental treatment ingredients that I value tremendously, ingredients that I see at the heart of growth and development in psychotherapy. Without empathy, without a sense of connection and psychological contact between therapist and client, there can be no therapy.

Clients who have experienced considerable rejection and hurt in their families of origin, rejection that has gone unacknowledged and unresolved, need a safe context within which they are given the opportunity to experience relationships in new ways. When safety and security characterize the therapeutic relationship, such interaction may represent the client's first occasion to experience support, encouragement, and emotional vulnerability with an empathic other.

### *Over- Versus Underchallenging the Client*

For the clinician who values the therapeutic relationship in the treatment of clients with traumatic histories, challenging avoidant defenses is hard to do. Turning the avoidant client's attention toward attachment-related issues and patterns can be difficult to manage in a manner that does not strain the therapeutic relationship and does not jeopardize the client's sense of feeling understood. It is not so easy to challenge defensive avoidance in a manner that is both attuned to the client's experience and yet not irritating, too much for the client to handle, or appearing as though the clinician were following a personal agenda.

Activating attachment can be difficult to do in practice, to do in a way that values the therapeutic relationship, maintains empathic attunement, and connects with the client rather than overwhelms or controls him. In this chapter, we discussed a sizable body of research, pointing in the direction of challenging defensive avoidance, and we discussed a number of reasons why such an approach is thought to be effective. But, in practical terms, how does one do so without jeopardizing the therapeutic relationship?

When making attempts to challenge defensive avoidance, it is easy to fall into a pattern in which the clinician, acting on his countertransference, particularly feelings of frustration with the client's defensiveness, becomes overly keen and aggressive and in the process *overchallenges* the individual. Out of such interchanges arise empathic failures and ruptures in the therapeutic alliance, along with temporary increases in symptomatology and possibly retraumatizing interactions. The client feels misunderstood and frustrated and becomes all the more convinced that therapy is not for him. And, because his pattern of dealing with relational distress is to minimize, he may not even be aware of or communicate feelings of dissatisfaction to the clinician, opting instead not to show up for subsequent appointments and then to convince himself that "things are just too hectic right now for therapy," burying feelings about the interpersonal conflict in the process. Therefore, an important aspect of the work with this population is in challenging defensive avoidance and activating the attachment system but *at a pace that the client can tolerate.* That is, gauging the individual's level of anxiety and working at a level that his anxiety can bear.

Of course, when empathic failures occur (and they invariably do), they can actually provide useful—albeit painful—opportunities for growth. For the client, the opportunity to discuss how he felt misunderstood by the therapist may present one of the first times he has actually taken such an emotional risk with anyone, perhaps expressing feelings, positive and negative, that he never before felt comfortable expressing. Naturally, this sort of interchange can only occur if the therapist has done the alliance-building work early in the treatment, is in the habit of recognizing countertransference, is open to noticing how her own behavior may have hurt rather than helped the client in the previous sessions, and in a nondefensive way is inclined to open up discussion of such relationship ruptures in subsequent sessions.

Thus, overchallenging the client represents a potential pitfall in attempting to activate attachment and challenge defensive avoidance. Similarly, an emphasis in the other direction, in which the clinician is overly cautious, can be problematic in its own right. And, the clinician may fall into a pattern that *underchallenges* the client.

Lifelong patterns of avoidance are powerful, and the therapist working with any individual in emotional distress, especially one with a high-risk history, is repeatedly pulled in the direction of "not imposing," not wishing to further the client's pain. The pressure not to discuss the elephant in the room can be powerful. In both the clinical literature and practice, therapists tend to characterize working with clients who avoid attachment as a stressful, laborious experience.

Sessions may seem emotionally anemic, or dull to sit through, as the client may wish to discuss anything but the issues that make her feel so vulnerable. The therapist may experience the hour as "empty" or "like pulling teeth," often circling around matters that appear to lack substance or repeatedly finding questions or interventions stifled and dismissed.

When questions or empathic comments are repeatedly shut down or when individuals insist on discussing issues that lend themselves to less distress, a common tendency is to accommodate.[5] This is natural. If not, the interaction would feel awkward, and conversation would not flow. However, the consequence of such accommodation is a co-constructed avoidance, one of which the therapist may or may not be aware. Importantly, some have argued (e.g., Steiner, 1993) that when there is too much of this kind of accommodation, the client may come to see the therapist as having given up or as feeling defeated. Or, the client may pick up on the dishonesty inherent in such a collusion.

For the therapist, the ability to catch himself overchallenging or underchallenging the client is a difficult but important aspect of treatment. There is a fine line to walk between these two alternatives. And, the ability to find that line is often a function of therapist countertransference. Over the next few chapters (Chapters 3, 5, and 6), we discuss similar issues that arise within the therapeutic relationship, issues that relate to both transference and countertransference.

Chapter 3 begins to examine specific approaches to intervention with this clinical population; some of these approaches I have described elsewhere (e.g., Muller, 2006, 2007, 2009; Muller, Bedi, et al., 2008). Bowlby (1988) stated that the therapist applying attachment theory helps the client explore representational models of self and of attachment figures with a view to reappraise and restructure them in light of new understanding. He acknowledged that the process can be a painful and difficult one, requiring the therapist to aid the

5. The tendency for clinicians to accommodate to client interpersonal expectations in treatment has been demonstrated in several investigations (see Daniel, 2006, for a review). In an outcome study by Hardy and colleagues (Hardy, Stiles, Barkham, & Startup, 1998) on the treatment of depression, the authors examined therapist use of varying levels of cognitive-behavioral and affective-relational interventions as a function of client pretreatment interpersonal style. They found that clients classified as "underinvolved" (comparable to avoidant attachment) tended to pull for more of the cognitive-behavioral and fewer of the affective-relational interventions. Similarly, clients classified as "overinvolved" (comparable to preoccupied attachment) pulled for the opposite (less-cognitive, more affective responses). Results demonstrated the notable effects of client interpersonal expectations on clinician responses in treatment.

individual in considering ideas and feelings about important others that had been previously regarded as unimaginable.

## Summing Up

How do we guide our approach to treatment if we expect to work from the standpoint of attachment theory and research?

In the beginning of this chapter, we described the three bodies of psychological research that point to a general treatment approach that favors activating the attachment system and challenging defensive avoidance. First, we discussed how individuals who are avoidant of attachment put considerable psychological effort into closing off discussion of threatening issues, and that unless we challenge deactivation, such issues will likely remain closed off. Next, we examined research findings on so-called noncomplementarity of attachment within clinician–client dyads in counseling relationships, and discussed studies that showed that clients who are avoidant of attachment do better in treatment when paired with therapists who have a bent toward a more activating pattern of attachment. Last, we looked at the phenomenon of defensive breakdown and noted how, among clients avoidant of attachment, defensive strategies such as deactivation are prone to fall apart when the individual is under attachment-related stress, and that such defenses are therefore associated with substantial health- and mental-health-related costs to the client.

In the second part of this chapter, we talked about how, practically speaking, it is not so easy to activate attachment and challenge defensive avoidance. We described a treatment paradox among such individuals. On one hand, we find a highly symptomatic presentation consistent with the client's high-risk history. On the other, we find a tendency toward help-rejecting defensiveness. In practice, the therapist ends up being pulled in opposing directions, toward acknowledging and focusing on client traumatic distress but, paradoxically, toward minimization and mutual avoidance of trauma as a way of accommodating to client expectations.

Mixed feelings about addressing traumatic experiences are inherent in the treatment paradox. Stemming in part from the client but transmitted to the therapist, such mixed feelings can pull the clinician into overchallenging or underchallenging the individual or even into a cycling back and forth, sometimes pushing too aggressively but sometimes sweeping traumatic events and attachment-related distress under the rug. So, when we consider the complexities of challenging defensive avoidance, we note that it is not always easy to do in a manner that protects the therapeutic relationship and keeps a healthy empathic connection between therapist and client. When we find this balance, we take part in a healing that is not only secure and safe but also honest.

CHAPTER 3

# Getting Started: Intervention Strategies

So far, we have looked at avoidant defensive patterns along with general treatment principles in relation to such patterns. We have also examined a guiding approach to ground our clinical work with this population in attachment theory and research. Let us now turn to specific intervention strategies that are necessary for the early phases of treatment, strategies that help the clinician get started.

Such approaches are intended to speak to the paradoxical nature of attachment avoidance among trauma survivors and address the mixed messages implicitly communicated by such clients from the beginning of the first therapeutic encounter. I refer to these strategies as addressing the "I'm-no-victim" identity, using symptoms as motivators, using ambivalence, and asking questions around themes of caregiving and protection.

## Addressing the "I'm-No-Victim" Identity

As presented in Chapter 2, one of the challenges in working with this population has to do with the conflict that arises between the reality of traumatic events and client self-perception; the striking contrast between the painful, traumatic experiences that have had an impact on the client's real life; and the individual's dominant identity of strength, self-reliance, and invulnerability.

From the start of treatment, the self-perception of the client who is avoidant of attachment renders much of the diagnostic language and terminology used by clinicians as off-putting. Common trauma-related language and jargon (e.g., post-traumatic stress disorder, adult survivor of abuse, victim of abuse, and so on) can make the individual feel uncomfortable as such labels contradict the usual way in which he sees himself. The words *trauma*, *abuse*, and *victim* all conjure up images of weakness and vulnerability. Phrases such as *survivor of abuse* have particularly negative connotations. And, emotional states associated with trauma, such as grief, sympathy, and self-pity, are all uncomfortable and contradict the dominant identity the individual has worked so hard to construct. In short, the client attempts to keep himself from being identified as a victim.

Many such clients tend to see people as either strong or weak and have tremendous difficulty understanding that there are shades of gray. Keeping the two worlds of strength and vulnerability separate requires a process of *splitting* one's personal life story in two. Such defensiveness keeps a very real and important aspect of one's life separated off and unexamined (Chu, Frey, Ganzel, & Matthews, 1999). It allows one to maintain a self-image of strength without having to face the pain of one's own vulnerabilities. Naturally, the effort required to sustain such a façade is substantial. When asked about memories of traumatic or even moderately painful events, when they are remembered, stories are told in highly distorted form (Freyd, 2001) or editorialized with comments like, "I don't want to turn this into some kind of 'pity party.'"

As an example, it is common that painful stories be recounted in the guise of light, humorous anecdotes. Let me turn to a case I worked on a few years ago. This 36-year-old presented with an unrelenting eating disorder that had persisted since early adolescence. Here, he described discipline in his family of origin:

---

I think once when we were like 6 years old, or something, or I'm 8 and my sister's 10, or whatever the case may be. And we were playing in the living room, and, like I guess, wrestling or whatever. We were jumping on the couch, and we knocked a lamp over, and everything over, and we were trying to clean it up quickly before my dad came. But he came, and he was mad. So he took off his belt. And we each got spanked. . . . I don't know how many times . . . but it didn't really hurt. And then we went out to the backyard. And we just laughed and laughed about it because we had candies stuffed into our back pockets, so it didn't even hurt. So it wasn't really that scary or anything . . . to me. We just thought it was funny.

---

In the early phases of his treatment, many such memories were recollected in highly distorted form. And, he was not at all critical of parental choice of discipline, working hard to convey to me that his father was in all respects flawless, in fact highly admirable.

Ironically, it is fairly common to hear such individuals state unapologetically harsh and unforgiving attitudes toward *other* victims, including a strong tendency to actually *blame* victims when they learn of others' abuse experiences. This is reflected in a rigidly applied ideology that minimizes the victim's experience and gives rise to judgments like: "They should get over it." Herman (1992) described the general tendency in society to find fault with the character of victims, criticizing them for showing inadequate courage or resistance or viewing them as having character flaws, and a number of research studies have looked at the phenomenon of victim blame, even the blaming of child survivors of abuse (e.g., Muller, Caldwell, & Hunter, 1994). However, of relevance here, it is often the client himself who holds such attitudes toward other victims.

The harsh language used by clients (who are avoidant of attachment) in relation to other victims often conceals the self-criticism that would arise if the individual were to view himself likewise. By keeping a self-image of strength and normality, as opposed to that of *victim*, the client protects himself from the vulnerability connected to having been victimized as well as from self-criticism for any perceived role he may have played in his own victimization. Equally compelling is the client's tendency to idealize an abusive parent, thereby protecting the relationship to the attachment figure (Davies & Frawley, 1994; Fairbairn, 1943/1952), often redirecting anger and blame away from the parent and toward others, such as siblings.

### *What Not to Do*

In psychotherapy, it is important not to make overly eager attempts to reconcile discrepant story lines or to precipitously get the client to "face reality" in a manner that feels obvious or forced, to push the client in an aggressive or irritating way into facing whatever painful events or emotions are being avoided (Sable, 2000).

It is not helpful to encourage too strongly the trauma survivor label, especially early in therapy. The client will patently reject the labels of "abuse" or "survivor." Even empathic statements that are intended to be supportive of the client's likely experience regarding traumatic events are often dismissed in early sessions. And, the individual is bound to leave the office feeling frustrated and misunderstood. Certainly, statements communicating that the person is "in denial" never work. It is also unhelpful, early on, to "educate" the client on what constitutes a history of abuse or trauma: how those with trauma histories often protect the abuser or on how trauma has negative effects on adult functioning. Again, the client will easily dismiss these ideas as not being applicable in this case.

## *What to Do*

### *Narrative Discrepancies*

In attempting to address the "I'm-no-victim" identity, what the therapist can do is to notice and draw attention to the narrative discrepancies found in the personal stories recounted by the client. That is, the therapist shines light on the ways in which different elements of the individual's personal stories do not add up; not in a manner that appears obvious or forced but rather in a collaborative, reflective way.

The clinician may invite the individual to make meaning of such apparent discrepancies, asking about what the possible connections may imply. However, it is important not to take the opportunity to "prove" the existence of such discrepancies. Instead, the stance the clinician adopts is one of curious exploration (Pearlman & Courtois, 2005), asking the client what he makes of the seeming inconsistencies in his personal story.

Such narrative discrepancies often occur across the personal stories told from session to session or even within a single session. For example, let us consider an individual who, early in treatment, describes his childhood as "totally normal" and "nothing unusual," with few examples to illustrate this perception. A few weeks later, the same individual may parenthetically mention how his mother used to discipline him with regular beatings using an electrical cord. Note that this might be presented as "no big deal" in the context of discussing some other matter. The therapist, careful not to overreact, adopts an unassuming stance and invites the client to grapple with the coexistence of these two ideas, perhaps saying something like, "I notice that when we first met, you described having a 'totally normal' childhood; is this event an example of that, or is this different in some way?"

The first time I point out a narrative discrepancy, I generally expect the client to respond relatively defensively, attempting perhaps to fit stories together without altering the glowing view of childhood. Such a response might look something like, "Well, I think it *was* normal because that's what everyone did back then. It's not like today. Besides, it's not like I was abused or anything."

However, as the therapeutic relationship develops and as the therapist conveys a safe, nonjudgmental interpersonal stance, it becomes increasingly likely that a question like the one posed by the clinician can be met with a response such as: "Well . . . this was different because my mom only did that when she had a little too much to drink. But, otherwise, it *was* totally normal. I mean . . . she's from Glasgow; they *all* drink [laughs]." A response like this, while still defensive in tone and still oriented toward protecting the parent, opens the door a crack to the idea that not everything was so rosy. And, with that come a host of follow-up questions, which have the purpose of broadening the client's otherwise narrow characterization of his childhood, questions that get at nuance and difference. Questions like, "Okay, I see what you mean. So, could you tell me a bit more about the ways it was *most* normal, and some of the ways it was *least* normal." Or "Was alcohol the only thing that could get your mom to behave not so normal, or was there anything else?"

Examining narrative discrepancies helps build shades of gray into the client's understanding of his story and in so doing begins to soften the person's need to so emphatically deny a view of self as vulnerable. It should be noted that specific answers to such questions are far less important than the simple act of reflecting on and wrestling with these issues, something that is normally done only on extremely rare occasion (e.g., briefly when emotionally touched by some external event, such as a movie).

Narrative discrepancies may also be detected when there is a palpable difference between the emotional tone of story and storyteller, in other words, when the emotional tone of the story does not match with the emotion being conveyed by the client. Let us turn again to the person who early in treatment described his childhood as "totally normal" but then later said something about how his mother used to discipline him with regular beatings using an electrical cord. This description might be told in such a manner that it neutralizes any painful emotion; for example, the client may recount the story as a humorous anecdote. The therapist listening to this may feel an uncomfortable pull in two separate directions: There is a pull to laugh because the usual social expectation is that if someone tells you something that he perceives as funny, you laugh or chuckle. Yet, at odds is a pull to empathize with the character in the story, who undoubtedly would feel pain and distress. As this occurs, the therapist may think, "I'm smiling, but it feels like a forced smile," or "Why on earth am I smiling?" This emotional discomfort is an important signal to the clinician that there is a narrative discrepancy at play. In this case, there is an emotional incoherence coming from the client that the clinician is picking up on.

As the treatment develops, the therapist draws attention to such patterns, again by shining light on the inconsistency and asking about it with interest. For example, "As you told that story, you looked like you found it really funny. Is that the *only* thing you were feeling?" This may be followed with, "Have you *always* found that to be a really funny story, or have you ever felt differently about it?"

Again, examining such narrative discrepancies helps build shades of gray into the client's understanding of his own narrative. In this case, the process of bringing to light alternate perspectives on the same story opens the door to experiences and feelings that are usually uncomfortable and out of view.

### *Keeping Focused on Attachment*

Because avoidance of attachment is largely about turning attention away from difficult emotions surrounding close relationships, it is important that gentle but consistent pressure be kept up to help the client stay focused. One of the hardest things I find about working in this area is in resisting the temptation to rescue (Pearlman & Saakvitne, 1995) the individual from the anxiety surrounding thoughts and feelings about terribly painful relationships and experiences.

When narrative discrepancies are highlighted, the client is being asked to grapple with issues that raise enormous discomfort. In such circumstances, it is common for the individual to give the knee-jerk response, "I don't know. I never thought about that before," and then look at the clinician, uncomfortably shifting back and forth between eye contact and looking away. Or, the client may search for a distraction or a change of topic. Or, she may respond in a terse manner, giving the nonverbal cue, "I have answered your question. Now it is time for you to come up with a different question." And, by answering the question briefly, the nonverbal message is communicated, "My answer was brief, so drop this topic!" It is easy for the therapist to feel a natural pull to rescue the client because in any normal social interaction that is exactly what one would do. Usually, we do not let conversations die or go flat or become terribly uncomfortable.

Instead of rescuing the individual with another question—one that is less threatening—what the clinician can do is directly ask the client to take her time and to think about it right now, even if it is the first time she has ever considered it. This is then followed by silence, a period of attentive, engaged silence, in accordance with the amount of anxiety the client can bear. This intervention seems relatively straightforward but is actually quite difficult to follow through because so many defensive maneuvers can be applied to draw the clinician back to rescuing the individual. When carried out, such an approach undermines the defensive process and is therefore experienced by the client as quite challenging. For the therapist, it may feel equally uncomfortable. However, it is only through such a process that the clinician communicates that therapeutic conversations are built on an honesty that is sometimes painful for everyone.

As described, such conversations are quite foreign to the client, so periods of silence should be expected. It is important that the therapist tolerate and use the silence, even when it may feel stressful to do so. Using silence in this way can be valuable as a therapeutic vehicle. While it raises anxieties, it also communicates to the individual that out of painful self-reflection can come new understanding. Kaner and Prelinger described silence in psychotherapy as a tool, noting that "silence can be used in place of words when all words fall short, such as during intense grief" (2005, p. 263). However, the authors also noted that, at times, it can be difficult:

> Silence can provoke anxiety. In ordinary social interaction, on television, radio, the phone, or at a cocktail party, silences are generally avoided for that reason. (p. 263)

When asking the client to engage in therapeutic conversations that feel foreign and stressful, it is helpful to debrief with the individual afterward, not in an obvious or mechanical way, but in a way that is true to the client's experience in the moment. Questions that ask about the experience of having engaged in difficult self-reflection are often meaningful to the client, and they help build further connections within the therapeutic relationship. After all, in this scenario, the therapist did, in fact, just ask the person to engage in a task that was emotionally risky and stressful.

I find it helpful to ask debriefing questions such as, "What was it like to be asked about something you had never thought about before?" or "What was the hardest part about being asked to think about that?" Such questions can open the door to the client saying something about her experience of you, her fears of being judged or scrutinized by you, and possible anxieties about what you expect of her. Recall that avoidance of attachment has its roots in experiences of rejection from attachment figures. Thus, any discussion that can open the door to the expression of fear of rejection in relation to the therapist can be enormously helpful later when the therapeutic relationship becomes a more direct instrument in the treatment.

## Clinical Overview Points

Do's and Don'ts in Addressing the I'm-no-victim Identity

DON'T:

- Make it your goal to "break through denial."
- Use trauma-related terminology or labels in relation to the client early in treatment.
- Let the client get away with responding "I don't know" to uncomfortable attachment-related questions without pushing back a bit.

DO:

- Draw attention to narrative discrepancies, stories that do not add up:
  - Discrepancies from session to session
  - Discrepancies between emotional tone of story and storyteller
- Use narrative discrepancies to develop shades of gray in the client's understanding of her own story.
- Use your own feelings as a signal that a narrative discrepancy is at play.
- Keep the client's focus on attachment-related issues.

- Allow for silence as the client struggles with painful attachment-related experiences or feelings.
- Debrief with the client after you have asked the individual to engage in stressful self-reflection.

## Using Symptoms as Motivators

Regardless of one's prior history, the actual decision to come for psychotherapy often occurs at a time that defenses have broken down in the here and now (Pearlman & Courtois, 2005). Trauma theorists (e.g., Gelinas, 1983; Herman, 1992) refer to the "disguised presentations" that bring individuals into treatment, especially those with histories of childhood abuse. Judith Herman (1992) wrote:

> They come for help because of their many symptoms or because of difficulty with relationships, problems in intimacy . . . and repeated victimization. All too commonly, neither patient nor therapist recognizes the link between the presenting problem and the history of chronic trauma. (p. 123)

At the point of making the decision to enter into treatment, coping resources are usually overextended (Sable, 2000), and the individual experiences everything as overwhelming. In practical terms, this means that several areas of the person's life are often affected. Typically, this includes problems at school that have spilled into both academic and interpersonal domains, struggles at work, complaints regarding social relationships, arguments or tense relations with spouses or partners, and child-rearing difficulties. Dozier and Bates (2004) indicated that clients who are avoidant of attachment often seek therapy because of loneliness and alienation. These are often accompanied by symptoms of depression, isolation, and anxiety.

This period of distress can give rise to an enormous opportunity for self-examination and change, although it certainly does not feel that way at the time. Most often, the individual just wants the symptoms to go away, and although psychotherapy may seem like something out of the norm, the client is willing to give it a try, having heard about counseling or therapy from a friend or relative. She may even have received a referral or two from the family doctor, who noticed and asked about stress-related symptoms. It is not uncommon to have held onto such referrals for months prior to making the decision to call or to ask others to place the call, putting some distance between oneself and the process. In this way, the path by which the client comes to therapy frequently occurs with much reservation.

### *Initial "Buy-In"*

Ironically, there is some advantage to this period of defensive breakdown in terms of therapeutic opportunity. That is, the presence of symptoms gives rise to an initial "buy-in" to psychotherapy. A pattern of noticeable symptomatology gives the client a reason to admit that help is necessary and provides justification for engaging in therapy, something that would be unthinkable if things were moving along as usual. This justification is critical to get the client through the door because, the majority of the time, individuals who are avoidant of attachment spend little time thinking about relationships, emotions, and psychological factors that affect their everyday lives. Without such situational distress, it would be easy to continue along that trajectory without much reflection or opportunity for change.

### *Making Symptoms Meaningful*

Early in treatment, it is important to help the client make a motivational shift from simple symptom relief to one in which psychotherapy starts to feel important on a deeper level (West, Sheldon, & Reiffer, 1989), a shift in which the person begins to experience a more meaningful connection to the process.

If the individual's motivation for psychotherapy stays at the level of simple symptom relief, he may become rapidly disillusioned with the process, terminating treatment long before being done. One reason for this is that symptoms often dissipate temporarily once therapy is initiated, during the proverbial "honeymoon" period. And, within a relatively brief period of time, the client may experience a certain measure of symptomatic relief. So, it is tempting for people who avoid attachment simply to drop out on the grounds that they are starting to feel a bit better. In fact, this temporary relief may even start as soon as the individual makes the decision to book the first appointment.

In part, this burst of positive gain early in treatment may be due to the simple, but transient, relief that comes with the feeling of having an important ally on one's side. That is, there are direct symptomatic benefits to experiencing an increase in social support (McLewin & Muller, 2006). And, the feeling of being supported by a therapist and other benevolent authority figures has been found in a number of studies to buffer the effects of stress on psychopathology. In part, as well, this burst of positive gain early in treatment may be attributable to the fact that the client has finally made a decision to do something about his difficult life situation. For many such individuals, a certain measure of relief comes with the idea that they are now addressing the problem.

However, as mentioned, if motivation for psychotherapy stays at the level of simple symptom relief, the client will drop out of treatment soon after a period of feeling a bit better. To address this problem, the therapist can make use of two techniques that operate side by side. These may be thought of as clarifying motivation and connecting symptoms to attachment.

### *Clarifying Motivation*

As discussed, individuals with histories of intrafamilial trauma rarely come to treatment to focus on the hurtful past when their usual way of dealing with attachment-related distress is through the use of avoidance. Instead, clients enter into the process on the grounds that they are symptomatic. When such "disguised presentations" (Gelinas, 1983; Herman, 1992) bring the individual into treatment, it is helpful to invite the client to clarify his motivation for psychotherapy.

Much has been written about "motivational interviewing" (e.g., Miller & Rollnick, 2002) and its usefulness in the assessment and treatment process to examine and clarify the individual's readiness for change in psychotherapy. Such clarification is particularly important for clients who avoid attachment. If the individual has been in treatment before, the therapist should ask about the course of that treatment and should take careful note of the reasons it ended. Often, the clinician will discover a checkered pattern of false starts or on-again, off-again treatments that were disrupted early for reasons unclear to the client.

It is helpful to ask the individual to reflect on why the previous treatment ended. What did he find most difficult about therapy? Why would this time be different? If the client has not been in therapy before, why enter it now? What has changed? Why would therapy help now? Many clients who avoid attachment will respond in global, impressionistic, stereotypic ways with goals like, "I don't want to be so negative all the time," without any clear justification. It is helpful to take the opportunity to gently challenge the client as to why. What is in it for them to "stop being so negative"? What might they gain, and what might they lose? And then, why stick with something like therapy if it makes you talk about the negative things in life?

Clarifying motivation can sow the seeds for later discussion of the individual's usual pattern of avoidance. It encourages the client to articulate his motivation to engage in a process like psychotherapy, which is something that is both challenging and out of the ordinary. Whatever the motivation for change, it can be referred to at a later time if the client does, indeed, propose to drop out precipitously. Interestingly, however, it has been my experience that by simply putting the question of motivation in full relief and asking the client to reflect on the matter, the individual becomes clearer regarding his motivation for treatment, and dropout itself becomes less likely.

### *Connecting Symptoms to Attachment*

*Connecting symptoms to attachment* refers to the idea that the therapist helps the client explicitly connect symptoms to psychologically meaningful reasons for treatment. This is not to belittle the importance of symptom relief per se. As mentioned, initial buy-in to psychotherapy is greatly facilitated by motivation for symptom relief. However, as described, if the stated motivation for treatment stays exclusively at that level, it is easy for clients, whose natural tendency is to avoid attachment, to drop out once symptoms dissipate even slightly.

Early in the process, the therapist should make use of symptoms to help such clients find a much more meaningful connection to psychotherapy. One way is for the clinician to draw a connection between symptoms and attachment-related issues. The therapist does this by asking about the relationship-based themes in the initial pattern of symptom presentation. Doing so helps the client recast symptom-based problems and goals into relational ones. Thus, the individual who allows himself to make the shift from viewing the problem as "depression and loneliness" to that of "self-isolation" or to that of "keeping people at arm's length" is far more likely to find psychotherapy meaningful.

It is important to note that making these connections should not be something that feels artificial or contrived. With such clients, there is a natural tendency to keep intimacy and feelings of vulnerability at bay. The clinician is helping by drawing attention to the attachment-related themes that are there but not currently in full view.

The connection between symptoms and attachment-related issues is facilitated by a line of questioning that asks about the effects of one on the other:

What is the effect of _____________ on _______________________?
(symptom) (relevant attachment theme)
What is the effect of _______________________ on _____________?
(relevant attachment theme) (symptom)

In practice, this may look something like, "How has depression affected your relationship with Paul?" or "How has your engagement to Paul affected your depression?" Or perhaps, "How did the performance anxiety affect your decision to have children?" or "How did fear of having children affect your performance anxiety?" Again, the answers themselves are less important than the process of engaging in the task of making meaning of symptoms. Being asked to think about symptoms in this way can be new and disquieting. However, some clients will respond fairly quickly with something that suggests that they may have entertained such ideas before.

One client I worked with when I was still in training had experienced one of the uglier histories of domestic violence I had come across at the time. When she was a child, she lived in abysmal conditions, including abject poverty. Her father had terrorized the family, often humiliating her mother to the point of making her eat dog food in front of the children as a show of submission. As an adult, my client hated everything about people who were weak (completely unaware that becoming like her mother was what terrified her). She arrived to one of her earlier sessions incensed by her boyfriend's accusation that she was "insanely independent." Although defensive at first, in time she was able to acknowledge that, indeed, this was a problem for her, but she did not know why. In fact, she confessed that she often felt "smothered" and "latched onto" by her boyfriend, the only romantic partner in her history who *never* physically abused her, and she found that paradox a bit strange as well. Soon, she came to view her depression as closely tied to "insane independence," and psychotherapy became increasingly focused on gaining greater understanding of this repetitive pattern in her life.

To recap, the presence of symptoms gives rise to an initial buy-in to psychotherapy. And subsequent meaningful connection of symptoms to attachment-related experience makes continued engagement in therapy that much more compelling.

### *Dismissing Disillusionment*

Related to the distress caused by symptoms in and of themselves is a certain emotional injury that goes along with having become symptomatic in the first place, a process I refer to as *dismissing disillusionment.* As the term suggests, when they become symptomatic, clients who are avoidant (dismissing) of attachment tend to experience a profound sense of feeling disillusioned (see also Muller, 2009; Teitelbaum, 1999).

As detailed in both the clinical and experimental literatures (e.g., Berant et al., 2001; Edelstein, 2007; Edelstein & Gillath, 2008; Muller, 2007, 2009), individuals who are avoidant of attachment are able to cope effectively with the ups and downs of life as long as attachment-related distress is kept to a minimum. But, when avoidant defenses no longer work effectively and clients become symptomatic, they find themselves shocked that they are no longer holding it together as they used to, asking themselves, "Why can't I handle things anymore?" Their current symptomatic state contradicts their proclaimed self-image, so they become disillusioned. One client put it succinctly following an out-of-character suicide attempt. As she forced a wide toothy smile, with eyes welling up, she insisted, "But I am a happy person! So, why am I *crying* all the time?"

#### *Using Disillusionment as a Motivator*

This sense of feeling disillusioned is distressing. However, the therapist can connect with the client by noticing it when it arises and by allying with the individual's motivation to understand why she would be feeling so much worse than before. Given the tendency toward strength and self-reliance, such individuals feel considerable disappointment in themselves for becoming symptomatic. There is a sense of personal failure and humiliation or anger at themselves for "falling apart" and a desire to figure out how to protect themselves from falling apart in the future. Strong emotions and sentiments such as these can be highly motivating, and the therapist can ally with the client, using her sense of disillusionment productively as a motivating force in the service of the therapy.

For one such client, who saw herself as "tough" and "level headed," her unmanageable feelings surrounding an inexplicable, out-of-character, 3-month drinking binge reportedly made her feel a sense of outrage, anger, and disappointment in herself and served as a motivator in psychotherapy as she wanted to keep something like that from ever happening again.

### *Focusing on Themes of Vulnerability*

As mentioned, the therapist connects with the client by noticing the disillusionment and by allying with her motivation to understand just why she would be feeling so much worse than before. In doing so, the clinician can ask about and listen for the meaning attached to symptoms. When such meanings suggest themes of vulnerability, these are pointed to, asked about, and discussed.

When individuals have experienced histories of trauma, particularly when suffering comes at the hands of those trusted most, there is a painful awareness of the price to be paid for excessive vulnerability. Vulnerability can mean weakness and may be frightening and dangerous. Avoidance of attachment is the pursuit of invulnerability, the pursuit of an illusion[6] that offers strength, reassurance, and a promise of safety. Part of the reason the client feels so profoundly disillusioned when she becomes symptomatic is that she has become painfully aware, again, of the harsh reality of her human weakness and all the dangers that go along with it.

An important component of the treatment process is in helping the client gain greater acceptance of her vulnerabilities (Sable, 2000), integrating them into her overall sense of self, so that they can eventually feel less dangerous and frightening. In fact, this will become an ongoing theme throughout the therapy because vulnerability is a fundamental prerequisite for intimacy. However, even early in the treatment, themes of vulnerability can begin to be examined when the individual expresses feelings surrounding having become symptomatic.

For example, consider the person who declares "spinelessness" as his word to describe the meaning of depression to him. This word can be contrasted

6. The psychological meaning of *illusions*, including their development, their usefulness as organizing principles, and the loss felt when they come apart, has been detailed in the writings of Teitelbaum (1999).

with the individual's more usual backdrop of, say, self-proclaimed strength. The therapist and client can then reflect on this vulnerability. The clinician inquires about its history in the person's life. "When was the first time you showed anyone your spineless side?" "On those rare occasions that it occurred, how did your parents deal with such spinelessness on your part?" "How have you reacted to spinelessness in others?" "How is it that your sister got the opportunity to be spineless, while you had to keep your spine so strong?"

As mentioned, specific answers to questions are far less important than the process of self-reflection. Recognizing feelings around having become symptomatic and then connecting them to other experiences of vulnerability helps the client integrate a far more textured and realistic view of self, a view in which stories of strength and weakness, independence and spinelessness, can come to coexist.

One of my clients, who presented with symptoms of bingeing to the point of physical pain, told me that in her view bingeing was a sign of "weakness." A physically fit, well-toned karate instructor, she was self-disciplined in every aspect of her life, depending on no one but herself. When asked to reflect on the various areas of her life in which she could show weakness, she noted that other than bingeing there were none. She was humiliated by her symptoms, and during her 18-month marriage that ended just 1 year prior to starting therapy, she had kept her weekly binges a tightly held secret from her husband, carefully removing empty cartons of ice cream before they could be discovered. Nevertheless, in the process of opening up, several months into the treatment she came to the realization that as much as she felt utterly demoralized following the binges, they were, in fact, the only context in her life in which she would dare to "lose control." Being able to give up control was something she wished she could do more of, especially because sexual pleasure and the ability to achieve orgasm had been such a problem for her throughout her brief marriage.

It is noteworthy that the process of examining themes suggestive of vulnerability may yield feelings such as anger and anxiety in relation to the therapist, especially early in treatment. After all, the individual's attention is being turned toward his uncomfortable emotional needs, and such exposure may feel humiliating. David Wallin, looking at attachment principles and patterns in psychotherapy, has pointed out that with clients who are avoidant of attachment, empathic attunement can backfire at times, with clients compelled to reject therapist comments because they evoke "multiple threats associated with closeness and dependency" (2007, p. 213). Heartfelt, accurate, empathic statements regarding traumatic experiences, which would be meaningful to most clients, may elicit unfavorable responses or may inexplicably fall flat. However, triggering the client's anxieties over dependency can also present a valuable therapeutic opportunity (West et al., 1989), the chance to explore the experience of appearing vulnerable in the presence of an important other.[7] These and related issues are discussed more fully in Chapter 5 in the exploration of client feelings toward the therapist.

## Clinical Overview Points

Things to Remember in Using Symptoms as Motivators

- Take note of initial buy-in that has been prompted by the presence of symptoms.
- Clarify motivation for psychotherapy:
  - Ask the client to reflect on her reasons for taking on therapy given that it raises uncomfortable, difficult feelings.
- Help the individual make connections between symptoms and attachment-related issues (to further strengthen motivation for therapy).
- Notice client disillusionment (over having become symptomatic):

7. Wallin argued in favor of letting avoidant clients in on the therapist's own experience of the relationship as such self-disclosure is thought to provide a route to "otherwise inaccessible feelings, thoughts, and memories" (2007, p. 213). In the context of a well-developed therapeutic relationship, such an approach may have the advantage of giving rise to a therapeutic climate in which vulnerability is seen as more acceptable in the presence of another, as the therapist herself is taking an emotional risk, making it that much less threatening for the client to do likewise. However, such an approach may also yield the unintended consequences of stirring both the client's defensive contempt for others' vulnerabilities and anxieties surrounding the ability of the therapist to be "strong enough" to rely on. Certainly, the strength of the therapeutic relationship would likely play a pivotal role in deciding whether to carry out such an intervention. In Chapter 5, we look further at vulnerability and the importance of the therapist taking an emotional risk in relation to the client, but doing so by openly addressing closeness/distancing patterns that occur between them in the therapeutic relationship.

- Ally with the individual's motivation to understand why she would be feeling so much worse than before.
- Be curious about and examine the meaning of symptoms that are suggestive of themes of vulnerability.

## Listening for, Noticing, and Using Ambivalence

One of the challenges in working with this population is determining what to do about client reluctance to face personal traumatic events. Even in the case of severe parental abuse or neglect, there is a strong tendency for such individuals to idealize one or both parents and to paint portraits that do not fit with the facts of their own stories[8] (Dozier & Bates, 2004; Hesse, 1999), leaving the therapist with the impression that the person is fooling himself. Traumatic events are minimized or made more socially appropriate (Slade, 1999), or a positive "spin" is placed on trauma stories, so that everything turns out all right in the end. These patterns are observable because stories do not fit together in a coherent fashion, and potentially threatening facts that are offered up in one context are recanted in another. No attempt is made to reconcile the discrepancy. Indeed, there is no detectable awareness of the discrepancy.

### *When Traumatic Thoughts and Feelings Get Triggered*

As noted, some things are hard to avoid indefinitely. The very nature of traumatic events is such that, over time, they are bound to get triggered (Wilson & Lindy, 1994). In describing the process of deactivation, Bowlby (1980) noted that the exclusion of significant information may be less than complete, and that there are times when "fragments of information defensively excluded seep through" (Bowlby, 1980, p. 65). Experiences such as intrafamilial trauma affect

8. I have sometimes been asked by supervisees whether idealization ever comes across as "gushy" or excessively "flattering" of the parent. Usually, it does not. Rather, it is more typically marked by the fact that there is a striking *absence* of criticism of a parent whom the therapist understands as clearly having been harsh, punitive, or abusive. This phenomenon is often evident when the client tells of aggressive, cruel punishment, offers no criticism, and quickly rationalizes the parent's behavior, perhaps adding a disconnected positive detail about him or her. The clinician is left with the impression that the client is somehow protecting the parent.

so many areas of psychological functioning that as individuals experience the ups and downs of life, trauma-related thoughts and feelings become increasingly unavoidable.

Among those clients who have experienced the more severe types of trauma, such thoughts and feelings are all the more difficult to avoid. Horowitz (1976, 2001) stated that warding off thoughts about traumatic events may alternate with intrusive repetitions across different relationships. When attachment-based life changes occur, these can often serve as triggers that destabilize the suppression of traumatic material. Such life changes include actual or perceived losses, medical illnesses, family crises, and important developmental shifts (such as anticipation of becoming a parent, of getting married, and so on). Sometimes, trauma-related thoughts and feelings can be triggered by external factors such as various forms of popular culture.

### *Ambivalence in Facing Trauma-Related Material*

When relevant interpersonal or intraindividual life changes occur, these can trigger thoughts and feelings related to traumatic experiences. When faced with such material, the client who is avoidant of attachment may, in part, rely on familiar coping patterns, such as minimization or denial. However, the nature of trauma is such that, in many respects, it is not so easy to avoid. So much has been written about trauma in popular literature and media that the individual may have begun to question himself about it even prior to starting therapy. Internal and external pressures to face trauma-related issues mean that at different points in time, the individual may present with characteristics of ambivalence, wanting or needing to discuss aspects of previous traumatic experiences but reluctant to do so out of anxiety or fear. Such moments of naturally occurring ambivalence can serve as windows of opportunity to move the therapy forward.

One such client, presenting with sexual difficulties and infertility, described years of sexual abuse by her older brother, with him also forcing her to perform sexual favors for his friends. Although she admitted that, as a child, she was often convinced her brother would eventually kill her, she characterized these experiences as irrelevant because she had "already dealt with them," describing them as "old news." When I inquired as to why she would bring the issue up at all if she felt it were irrelevant, she shrugged, "I don't know. Must be all the *Oprah Winfrey* I watch," jokingly referring to sexual abuse as an ongoing discussion topic on that television show. Following this, she promptly changed the subject.

For a while, she refrained from any discussion of the abuse, focusing instead on her panic disorder and poor organizational skills at work. Nevertheless, she came back to the topic in the session following her 40th birthday, when a friend told her that since she was 40, her difficulty becoming pregnant may now be a permanent condition. In one of her more emotional sessions, she confessed that if she could become a mother without having to endure sex, she would. After which, she asked me if I thought this sexual problem had anything to do with the years of sexual abuse by her brother. I replied with something as simplistic as, "I don't know. . . . What do you think?"

Her response to this common question was quite striking, expressing feelings related to her abuse history that came across as far more genuine than anything she had expressed before. She acknowledged, for example, that her parents had been quite unresponsive to the ongoing abuse, mostly ignoring it. Later in our work, she recalled that at age 14, when she finally told her mother about the sexual abuse, her mother demanded she immediately apologize to her brother for "spreading lies" about him. Such recollections were terribly frightening to her as it meant confronting her more usual tendency to idealize her childhood relationship with her parents. Nevertheless, this became something I could make reference to, ask her to make connections to, and encourage her to expand on in subsequent sessions.

In the case presented, the threat of lost motherhood in part served to help mobilize the client toward greater self-reflection. With such individuals, it is often during periods of attachment-based change and psychological transition that defenses become less rigid, and a window of opportunity opens. During such a time, the therapist can listen for and notice signs of naturally occurring ambivalence as it is in such a context that the client is most likely to reflect on and reappraise long-held ideas.

### *Therapist Feelings When Responding to Ambivalence*

The other side of client ambivalence is the piece the therapist brings to the table, that is, the extent to which the clinician turns the attention toward trauma-related material, and focuses in on it, when it naturally arises in the treatment (Dalenberg, 2000). The decision to pursue this material is often a difficult one to make. With clients in this population, when trauma-related references arise, they do so in a minimizing, vague, contradictory, or perfunctory manner. The individual often drops little details suggestive of traumatic events as he discusses something else altogether. In other words, trauma-related references often arise out of context.

The presentation of such "fragments" (Bowlby, 1980) creates a challenge for the clinician. She is left to make decisions regarding the extent to which she will focus in on such references, seek clarification or embellishment from the client, show special interest in such material, come back to trauma-related references made months earlier, make such material a focus of treatment even if the individual does not initially see that as necessary, and so on.

In such a case, the therapist is left holding the ambivalence that the client cannot tolerate holding himself. The "pull" is for the therapist to resolve this in the simplest and most comfortable manner by going along with what the individual is most obviously asking for (Bernier & Dozier, 2002). When the client minimizes the magnitude of the trauma, there is pressure on the therapist to do so as well. When the individual conveys dismissal of the therapist's questions regarding trauma, the therapist may naturally accommodate and adjust her questioning.

Clients who are avoidant of attachment often respond to questioning about trauma-related feelings by rejecting them outright, minimizing therapist observations, or using defenses such as intellectualization to dampen the intensity of the therapist's comments. In response, the therapist may react (Mills, 2005; Pearlman & Courtois, 2005) to such rejection or minimization with a variety of normal emotions (e.g., frustration, irritation, hurt, disappointment) depending on the clinician's personal history and attachment pattern (Dozier & Tyrrell, 1998; Gelso & Hayes, 1998; Mohr, Gelso, & Hill, 2005). However, as the therapy proceeds, the therapist may accommodate to the client by way of collusion (Wilson & Lindy, 1994), such that the topic of trauma continues to be unspeakable or severely watered down. As noted in the previous chapter, theorists have described countertransference with such clients as the tendency to engage in a "mutual avoidance" (Alexander & Anderson, 1994), which provides relief for both client and therapist (Davies & Frawley, 1994).

The challenge facing the therapist is to make active attempts to turn attention toward trauma-related material, to listen for it, notice it, ask about it, and to facilitate rather than avoid such painful topics (Slade, 1999). If not, the risk is that of replicating the rejecting response of the parent who reacts to the child's abuse revelations by discounting or minimizing their importance or of replicating the weak and incapable parent who cannot tolerate her child telling her about what is really going on without squelching the information, failing to react, overreacting, or falling apart emotionally.

To facilitate this process, it is helpful for the therapist to make active attempts to think about a variety of personal anxieties in treating this population. Countertransference reactions in the therapy are detailed in Chapter 6. However, here I would like to note that feelings the therapist experiences in response to the client have a strong impact on the decision to pursue or not to pursue trauma-related material as it arises naturally in the treatment. As mentioned, researchers Cohen and colleagues (2006) underlined the importance of the clinician becoming comfortable with hearing trauma-related stories, noting that even subtle reluctance and anxiety on the therapist's part are often communicated to the individual, and that the client often withholds telling the full story out of fear that the therapist might not be able to handle it.

Such reluctance on the clinician's part includes, among other things, anxieties about the act of unsettling things that could just as well be left alone, discomfort about "making waves" in interpersonal contexts, guilt about "causing" others pain and discomfort, reluctance to "intrude" on the privacy of others, a certain tendency toward "squeamishness" in thinking about the breaking of cultural taboos, and discomfort with all things repulsive, repugnant, and disturbing. Anxieties or hang-ups in any of these areas can make it difficult for the therapist to feel comfortable bearing witness to the client's painful story.

## Clinical Overview Points

Do's and Don'ts in Listening for, Noticing, and Using Ambivalence

DON'T:

- Collude with general reluctance to address traumatic experiences.

DO:

- Listen for and notice moments of client ambivalence in relation to traumatic experiences.
- Consider ambivalence to be a therapeutic opportunity.

- Take the opportunity to ask the client to reflect on and make meaning of traumatic experiences.
- Notice times you get pulled into colluding with avoidance.
- Think to yourself about what those times might say about *you*.

## Asking Questions Around Themes of Caregiving and Protection

By definition, clients who are avoidant of attachment are reluctant to turn their attention toward memories, thoughts, and feelings that remind them of early relationships. This makes it a challenge for them to engage in psychotherapy because virtually all modalities of therapy invite the person to take part in the act of self-reflection, reflection on problematic relationships, and the analysis of situations, thoughts, and feelings marked by interpersonal conflict.[9] One's reflections on such matters are necessarily informed by one's relational map. Clients who avoid looking at that map are bound to believe that psychotherapy is not for them.

Helping the individual find ways to talk about attachment-related thoughts and feelings can present a challenge for the therapist, especially early in the treatment process. However, theory and research in the field of attachment pro-

9. In a study by McBride, Atkinson, Quilty, and Bagby (2006), the authors looked at the effects of attachment patterns on treatment outcome in a randomized control trial of interpersonal psychotherapy (IPT) and cognitive-behavior therapy (CBT). The results indicated that outcome varied depending on attachment orientation, with avoidant individuals demonstrating greater reductions in treatment severity among the CBT group. Interestingly, in his analysis of the McBride et al. (2006) study, Eagle (2006) wrestled with the question of what accounted for the findings, noting that among other factors, CBT, which places emphasis on the causal role of dysfunctional cognitive processes, may challenge the cognitive system that deactivates relationship and attachment-related needs. In other words, helping the client examine his dysfunctional cognitions with respect to relevant interpersonal relationships may act in the service of activating the client's attachment system. Only a few CBT-oriented theorists (e.g., Liotti, 2007) have acknowledged the possible role that activating the attachment system may have in yielding positive outcome in CBT. However, regardless of the presumed mechanism of change in CBT (a question for which the jury is still out), Eagle's analysis underscores the point that many schools of psychotherapy focus on active self-reflection on attachment-related difficulties, and that in this act of self-reflection, disclosing one's suffering to an available person who is perceived as "stronger and wiser than the self" activates the attachment system (Liotti, 2007, p. 145).

vides some compelling possibilities. As described, Bowlby (1980, 1988) viewed attachment as a fundamental biologically based system oriented toward seeking protection from the caregiver, with attachment-related motivations representing survival value in humans. Researchers George and Solomon (1999) and Hinde (1982) proposed that the attachment system is but one of a number of behavioral systems that have evolved to promote survival, and that behavior is the product of the interaction among different behavioral systems. Working in concert with the attachment system is the caregiving system. George and Solomon (1999) detailed the reciprocity between attachment and caregiving, noting that the goal of attachment behavior is to seek protection. In complement, the goal of the caregiving system is to provide protection. Similar internal and external cues associated with fear and danger activate both the attachment and caregiving systems. When the caregiving system is activated, the individual calls on a host of behaviors whose goal is to ensure protection of the child (George & Solomon, 1999).

### *Why Ask About Caregiving and Protection?*

The psychological link between attachment and caregiving can be used strategically in individual psychotherapy. Helping the client focus on caregiving, particularly around themes of protecting others, can be clinically productive. The rationale is that, for such individuals, this approach is often highly motivating. It engages on ideas that are active rather than passive (Weiss, 1986), ideas that have a future orientation, ideas that are related to doing rather than being done to. The "victim" orientation, so distasteful to the client who is avoidant of attachment, assumes passivity and the inability to act. In contrast, "protecting" is an active concept and reflective of the wish to make things better. On the Adult Attachment Projective (George & West, 2001), for example, stories of active protection are considered to be reflective of the "capacity to act."

As noted, individuals who are avoidant of attachment have tremendous difficulty engaging in honest critique of their parents. Instead, they deny feelings of rejection or vulnerability and minimize the failure of their parents to provide adequate protection. Nevertheless, they are often willing to engage in discussion regarding the protection of others, such as romantic partners, their children, or even their imagined future children.

Of course, this is not to say that such clients are necessarily appropriately protective of their children in reality or provide adequate caregiving in their actual observable behavior. In fact, it is well known that avoidant attachment among parents represents a significant risk factor for insecure attachment among their children (Hesse, 1999). Rather, it is just to say that within the psychotherapeutic environment, the act of thinking about protecting others is one in which such clients are willing to engage and do so much more readily than the act of thinking about their own history of failed protection.

It is important to note that while stories of protecting others may come up in the domain of caregiving, they may come up in other domains as well, in ways that are less obviously connected. It is not uncommon to hear client stories of workplace experiences or of interactions with friends in which they figure as the one others came to in times of need, or the one who protected a colleague: the benevolent team leader, the one who stuck out his neck to protect a friend, or the one who gave money to the secretary whose child really needed it, and so on. It is often hard to know how accurate these stories are. Clearly, there is a certain bravado, a gratifying self-indulgence that goes along with protecting others, being the rescuer or savior. But, the reality is really of secondary importance here. For our purposes, what is of use in treatment is the knowledge that such stories are on the client's mind. The individual who is powerfully engaged by his role as a protector, through his actions and words, is trying to work something through, to somehow complete the protection that never came to pass in his own life, and in the process, he is attempting to undo the pain of his own traumatic history.

As an example, one client I treated for about 2 years, who had suffered severe emotional and physical abuse from his chronically mentally ill mother, originally came to see me for therapy unable to make a commitment to any of his three girlfriends, with whom he had fathered at least one child each. He was quite bright, yet limited emotionally, expressing little understanding of others' feelings. Although lacking much understanding of children and their psychological motivations, he nevertheless considered himself to be a "good father" who protected the financial security of his children. On his salary as a paramedic, he had managed to pay off a sizable portion of three separate mortgages on the three homes he would rotate between throughout the week to be with his different families.

Typically even keeled in therapy, his most emotional sessions would take place in the months following the abandonment of his 8-year old son, Matthew, by the boy's mother. Although initially reacting primarily to the crisis and situational factors (e.g., enlisting the daily help of his then-unemployed sister), over several months he came to speak of Matthew more often than not. He became deeply concerned with Matthew's well-being, focusing heavily on protecting him both at home and at school. In fact, in uncharacteristic form, he lost control and was angered at one parent–teacher meeting when he was told that Matthew might have a learning disability, feeling terribly worried about how Matthew might react to the news.

As stories of protecting others come up in the client's discourse, it is important that the therapist notice them and invite reflection on the meaning of protection in the person's life. Most importantly, it is critical to help the individual make a connection between protection outward and experience inward.

### *From Protecting Others to Looking Inward*

From the standpoint of treatment strategy, once reflecting on caregiving has been initiated and discourse on the act of protecting others has been opened, the client can start to make connections to his personal history. There will be some softening to the idea of looking inward. The therapist can then ask about similarities or differences between the client's experiences of protecting others and his experiences around being protected (or not) as a child. In the case presented, discussion of the client's protectiveness of Matthew yielded many fruitful connections to his own history, namely, his identification with Matthew, his own sense of abandonment in childhood whenever his mother would be psychiatrically hospitalized, and his guilt for failing to protect Matthew adequately in the first place.

It is important to note that the parallels between protecting others and the client's personal history of failed protection are most useful when drawn in emotional terms. Once the client was able to speak of his son Matthew as feeling "heartbroken" and how he desperately wished he could fix that for him, he was able to admit more freely to times in his own childhood when he wanted, more than anything else, to make that heartbroken feeling go away forever.

## Clinical Overview Points

Things to Remember in Asking about Caregiving and Protection

- Pay attention to themes of caregiving and protecting others in the client's life.
- Invite the client to reflect on the meaning around particular acts of protecting others.
- Help the client look at similarities/differences between protecting others and personal experiences around being protected (or not) as a child.

CHAPTER 4

# Facilitation of Mourning in Emotional Detachment

Attachment theory was born of complex human reaction to loss. Based on meticulous observation of children removed, for a time, from maternal care, attachment theory helped explain behavior that otherwise seemed difficult to comprehend. Individuals react to loss in ways that are complicated, sometimes self-defeating, and often counterintuitive to the observer. The walls that some put up in an attempt to protect themselves are the very ones that turn others away, making it difficult to penetrate, connect, and offer the emotional support the individual needs.

The practical application of attachment theory when working with emotional detachment is the main purpose of this chapter. As we will see, the facilitation of mourning is critical to the process. The tendency to distance oneself from the painful emotions associated with overwhelming loss is one of the central features of avoidant attachment. This is illustrated in the case that follows.

---

## *The Case of Alex*

Alex came to see me through a referral made by his family doctor, who had a particular interest in substance use and who knew of my interest in trauma.

For about 2 months before I started seeing him, Alex and his doctor had been working together on a weekly basis to address the client's alcohol and marijuana abuse. Reportedly, he had responded reasonably well to a direct, goal-oriented approach, reducing his intake to just a couple of drinks of beer or wine a night. His pot smoking also became more manageable, down to about half its former level, which had been as high as four joints a day.

At its worst, Alex's substance use had gotten to the point at which he would drink at least a bottle of wine every night and would spend almost all his time watching television. Much to his pregnant wife's frustration, he was unwilling to engage with her on any meaningful level, opting instead to spend his days either engrossed in video games or desperately trying to complete his master's thesis in philosophy, which never did seem to get done and which he could barely work on for more than one or two pages without ingesting something. In her second trimester of pregnancy, she felt anxious about his inability to "get his act together" and would often implore him to go get help.

His history of alcohol and drug use went some years back. He had often written his undergraduate exams and essays high on marijuana, finding them too stressful to complete otherwise. When he and his wife were first married, they would "party," both together and with friends, at least a few times per week. But once she graduated and began working in library administration at the university, his wife's interests changed, and she started to confront him on the extent of his drinking and pot smoking. Fed up, it was she who originally placed the call to the family doctor.

When Alex first came to see me, he had already been in treatment for about 2 months. With the help of his family doctor, he had made significant progress in reducing his alcohol and marijuana intake. Even though substance use continued to be a problem that we would address on and off, it was not the main focus of our work together. What Alex needed help with now were the symptoms of panic that began to appear following the birth of his son, symptoms that worsened over the 6 weeks that followed and became worse still as he actively reduced his drinking and pot smoking. We agreed early that Alex would continue to work with his family doctor around issues related to medication management as well as substance use, and Alex and I would focus more on his anxiety and panic, although he had already been told (by his family doctor) of the connection between anxiety and substance use and was willing to acknowledge that his tendency to use substances was a way of medicating himself.

Alex found the anxiety debilitating. Even simple tasks such as shopping, running errands, and making appointments overwhelmed him. On a few occasions, he had experienced full-blown panic attacks, including visits to the local emergency room, worried he was dying or having a heart attack, with the reassurances of the emergency room doctors only helping for a short time. He isolated himself from friends and family, much preferring contact by e-mail instead of talking in person or on the phone. Despite his wife's encouragement, he was too incapacitated to call his best friend on the friend's birthday, feeling "like an idiot" about it later.

He felt terribly disconcerted by his inability to do what were once mundane tasks, at times quite self-critical, referring to himself as "useless." And, he found it nearly impossible to concentrate on his philosophy thesis at all without becoming exceedingly anxious. Frustrated by the length of time his thesis was taking, he found some work in construction at a job site nearby, where there were relatively few demands, despite his wife's wishes that he complete his graduate training to pursue the academic career he had always hoped to have. In fact, Alex had been told by his mentors that he had considerable potential, having successfully copublished his undergraduate thesis with his major professor just a couple of years earlier.

In the first few sessions, I worked with Alex around clarifying motivation for treatment, inviting him to connect symptoms of anxiety to attachment-related issues (see Chapter 3), which he responded to reasonably well. He was able to agree that having a child had been stressful for him, and that getting some help around coping with becoming a parent could be useful to address in treatment. Further, he viewed himself as someone who had always been strong and reliable, acknowledging a sense of frustration and disappointment in himself that he was no longer able to cope as he once did, wishing to regain control as soon as possible and to understand why he fell apart. He was also distressed by his inability to "take care of" his young family, seemingly humiliated by his panic attacks, but reluctant to acknowledge such feelings directly.

To become clearer on his family history, in early sessions I questioned him regarding attachment-related childhood experiences. His initial response to this was, "It was all pretty good," explaining that he was taught early to take care of himself, citing as an example the time he broke his thumb while skateboarding at age 12 and how he was able to walk himself to the nearby hospital to get an X-ray. He considered his childhood to be typical, even "boring," stating that it was only in the 11th grade, once he read Ayn Rand's work on objectivism, that he had anything "meaningful to say."

As with many clients avoidant of attachment, he seemed to lack personal stories, often appearing more interested in describing his wife's childhood than his own, occasionally going off topic, necessitating clarification regarding whether he was discussing his childhood or hers. In fact, his manner of speech was notable in his reluctance to use the pronoun *I* when describing emotional situations, instead substituting the pronoun *you*. Thus, when asked about his feelings at the time of the childhood skateboarding accident, he answered, "You did what you had to back then," and "That's the way it was. You couldn't let the little things stop you." This reliance on generalized statements and platitudes using the pronoun *you* turned out to be one way in which he would sidestep personal questions related to painful experiences.

Despite his difficulties engaging in the interview process, we did get to the topic of important early losses. In a cool, detached manner, Alex described his first day back at school after Christmas vacation at age 6; how he walked home on his own at the end of the day and found his mother crying, unable to tell him why, and how irritated he felt with her. And how, later that evening, when his aunt was over, it was she who explained that Alex's father, a construction worker, had been killed that morning. Apparently, he was crushed by a garbage truck at a job site, as Alex said "squashed." I found it odd that he would use such a word in this context and wondered if, on some level, he was using a light and humorous word to keep from expressing more genuine feelings.[1]

I would find out in a later session that he missed most of that school year, being taken from one medical appointment to the next by his mother due to a variety of symptoms he was experiencing throughout that time, including stomachaches, nausea, and so on. I would also find out in later sessions that his mother went on to become depressed for the next 2 years, and that at the age of 8, it was Alex who cooked most of the family meals as his mother had become all but emotionally incapacitated, and that even with all the responsibilities he took on, he was still able to keep his grades up.

Nevertheless, it was only on reflecting on the story later that it had its true

1. A colleague commenting on this case noted the childlike nature of "squashed" and how suggestive the word was of Alex being stuck in the experience as it occurred at age 6. Indeed, to that point, Alex never had mourned the loss.

impact on me. During the session in which he told me of his father's death, a narrative discrepancy (see Chapter 3), one between emotional tone of story and storyteller, was operative. Recall that when this occurs, the emotional tone of the story does not match with the emotion being conveyed by the client. With Alex, I observed such a discrepancy at the time that he relayed his story; I felt touched by the circumstances of his father's death and his mother's inability to help him through it, but also uncomfortable by his emotional distance and his detached stance regarding the experience. More than anything, he seemed distant, bored, as though he were describing something minor that had happened to someone else. On occasion, he also appeared flippant, as though it did not mean all that much to him.

At the time he told his story, I felt both a sense of empathic distress on his behalf and the impression that he did not want to pursue this any further, making the interaction feel rather awkward. In a session that occurred several months later, once he began to feel somewhat closer to his experience of loss, he would describe feeling guilty at times, that he could not get himself to feel upset, that he knew he *should* be upset, but that something was stopping him.

## Emotional Detachment

Before looking at the ways in which Alex's story can help inform treatment, let us consider how attachment theorists have looked at emotional detachment.

### *Emotional Detachment in Children: Bowlby's Observations*

In his three-volume work on attachment and loss, Bowlby (1969/1982, 1973, 1980) described in great detail research findings on the effects of traumatic separations in children. He drew on observational data, reaching as far back as World War II, studies conducted at the Hampstead Nurseries by Dorothy Burlingham and Anna Freud (1974), as well as studies carried out during the 1950s and 1960s by his colleagues at the Tavistock Child Development Research Unit (e.g., Heinicke & Westheimer, 1966), including the observations and an influential film made by James Robertson (1952).

Critical to Bowlby's (1969/1982, 1973, 1980) understanding of normal attachment behavior and the effects of overwhelming separations were the behaviors of preschool children removed from maternal care. These were children staying for a time in hospital wards or residential nurseries, youngsters who had been removed from the people and environments most familiar to them, and cared for by strangers, for a couple of weeks or longer. Taking great pains to differentiate his work from his predecessors' by underscoring his use of prospective, rather than retrospective, observational method, Bowlby described a consistent pattern of behavior among such children, manifested on separation from primary attachment figures.[2]

Bowlby divided the patterns of behavior that these preschoolers displayed into three phases: protest, despair, and detachment. *Protest* referred to acute distress associated with unbearable loss. In young children, this meant crying, shaking, screaming, throwing themselves around, and searching for any signs that the parent had returned. After a time (between a few hours and several days), the child's behavior began to show evidence of increasing hopelessness. Referred to as *despair*, this phase included a tendency to withdraw, to become inactive, and to make few demands on others, with more intermittent crying. Finally, during the third phase, *detachment*, the child started to demonstrate more interest in his immediate environment. This included a greater willingness to accept food, care, and toys, as well as greater sociability and frequency of smiling. Bowlby noted that sometimes adults incorrectly came to believe that the child was now less distressed and showing signs of recovery. In fact, the child had not recovered. When the mother would visit, there would be a troublesome absence of normal attachment behavior. The child would seem distant, remote, uninterested in her, detached from attachment-related feelings and behaviors. And, in those children for whom the period of separation continued, detachment would become worse still, particularly if there was a succession of institutional caregivers. Describing the effects on youngsters, Bowlby observed that the child would become interested in material things such as candy and toys

2. Although Bowlby was referring to child behavior evident in response to separation from mothers particularly, it is also the case that his observations were made at a time when mothers, rather than fathers, were far more likely to have been responsible for all child care. In fact, children respond with attachment behavior to the adults (mother, father, grandparent) most available for caregiving and with whom the relationships are most central. Although mothers still avail themselves more often to caregiving and are more likely to bring children in for treatment, we now know that emphasis should be placed more on the nature of the attachment relationship and on the traumatic effects of disruptions to that relationship than on the gender of the caregiver per se.

and would stop showing feelings when parents would arrive and leave on visiting days; over time, the child would become interpersonally aloof. That is:

> He will appear cheerful and adapted to his unusual situation and apparently easy and unafraid of anyone. But this sociability is superficial: he appears no longer to care for anyone. (p. 28)

### *Emotional Detachment in Adults*

Using the term *affect phobia* to describe the tendency in some individuals to avoid internal affective states, McCullough and colleagues (Kuhn & McCullough, 2002; McCullough, 1998, 2001; McCullough & Andrews, 2001) explained that certain experiences and emotions are intolerable because of the conflicted feelings they arouse. Traumatic experiences are associated with difficult, complicated emotions. In addition to the expressed and unexpressed anger that clients feel toward those who have hurt them, there are a host of affective states of which the individual is often unaware: painful longing for what might have been, distress about having been abandoned by the person trusted most, and the wish to complete the relationship that was somehow derailed too soon.

Adults who are detached from their emotions are at a disadvantage when they meet attachment-related challenges in the interpersonal world. When relationships become close, emotional, or complicated, the individual is "afraid to allow himself to become attached to anyone for fear of a further rejection with all the agony, the anxiety and the anger to which that would lead" (Bowlby, 1979b, pp. 11–12).[3] Naturally, this makes it difficult for such clients to develop and maintain genuine relationships with others (Sable, 2000). The tendency toward self-sufficiency provides a sense of comfort and control. It ensures that relationships remain safe, and that feelings that represent vulnerability are kept at a distance. But, it can lead to an existence that is rather lonely. Even when they are able to enter into committed relationships, they have tremendous dif-

3. Modell (1975) described a similar process of defense against affects, drawing on some of the same psychoanalytic sources used by Bowlby (1973). Although Modell was theoretically focused on the treatment of narcissism in particular, Bowlby also noted that the emotionally self-sufficient client "may later be diagnosed as narcissistic or as having a false self of the type described by Winnicott (1960)" (1988, pp. 124–125).

ficulty taking emotional risks, and the barriers they put up ensure that they do not become vulnerable to hurt and rejection.

---

Alex and I had worked together for about a month when we began to discuss his general tendency to resist emotional overtures made by important others in his life. Prior to the treatment segment presented next, he had been discussing how he had difficulty whenever his son cried, and how it bothered him when his mother would call to ask if she could see her grandson. He also spent part of the session discussing conflicts between him and his wife, as well as conflicts with friends, one of whom knew about his breakdown and had left several messages asking how he was doing. In this segment, he begins by discussing his irritation with his friend.

*Alex:* Now, he doesn't ask me about it. I'm a pretty strong person, so people don't really want to have to deal with me. "If I didn't tell you about it, then don't ask me about it."
*R.M.:* And you're saying people get that message?
*Alex:* Yes, they do.
*R.M.:* Right [nods]. . . . The message being . . . ?
*Alex:* [looks puzzled]
*R.M.:* You said, "Yes, they do." The message they get from you is . . . ?
*Alex:* Uhm yes, the message being, uh, don't confront me about something unless I fee—unless you have something substantial to say or unless I come to you.
*R.M.:* Don't confront? Or don't even ask?
*Alex:* Don't even ask, er . . . I consider that confronting [shifts in chair].
*R.M.:* Confronting [nods] . . . mm . . . when your friends ask you what's going on for you personally, you consider that to be . . . confronting?
*Alex:* Yeah . . . umm . . . yes.
*R.M.:* Right [nods].
*Alex:* Yeah, I do.
*R.M.:* [nods]
*Alex:* Like maybe they don't realize it, but then they'll realize from my reaction. And then they won't . . . they usually won't do it again.
*R.M.:* Mm hmm [nods]. [pause, 3 seconds] . . . And, umm, how do you understand it, that you equate being asked about your feelings to being confronted?

*Alex:* [pause, 3 seconds] . . . Because, I don't, I don't think it's . . . you know . . . appropriate, like, you wouldn't say—if somebody, uh, if someone dies, if someone close to you, if somebody died [voice tightens], you wouldn't go up to that person and start asking how they *feel* about it, you just, you know, be there with that person, for that person, and if they feel the need to—I don't know . . . that's my philosophy, if they, if they need to talk about it, or you see they need to, you know . . . you accommodate them at that point, and . . . uh . . . [pause, 3 seconds] you know, yeah, I'm pretty, umm, I'm a pretty strong stance kind of person in all different kinds of respects. . . .
*R.M.:* Mmm [nods].
*Alex:* —So people, they don't, well, . . . [pause], try to get on my wrong side or whatnot . . . [trails off].
*R.M.:* Uh hmm [nods]. . . . And you've even said that your friends have said to you—
*Alex:* —Yeah—
*R.M.:* —You've gotten into arguments with Cliff and with Karen because they've said to you they want to understand more about what's going on for you inside, and that creates a conflict between you and them.
*Alex:* Yeah, it does.
*R.M.:* It's a tough situation for you when they want to know what you're feeling.
*Alex:* Yeah.
*R.M.:* Yeah [nods] . . . Mmm . . .

---

Alex's emotional constriction and avoidance to the point of pushing away those closest to him was evident here. As suggested, his tendency toward self-reliance provided a sense of control. It ensured that relationships remained free of possible hurt and rejection, and that feelings that represented vulnerability were kept at a distance.

## Mourning

To a great extent, trauma is about loss. In families in which the child has been subjected to physical or sexual abuse or neglect from parents or there is severe parental rejection, abandonment, or harsh criticism, there is a lost sense of caregiver protection, loss of childhood (Cloitre, Cohen, & Koenen, 2006), and loss of innocence. In relation to adults who have betrayed the trust of the child, in addition to hurt and anger, there is often a deep disappointment in caregivers, particularly when the child sees that others around her may appear to have very different kinds of families. If there is occasional regret expressed by a parent for past behavior, there may be a cycling of promises made and promises broken, which can lead to emotional cycling in the child between hope and disappointment. But, in the face of repeated parental failures, hope may seem lost as well.

In families in which caregivers have died or left the family (as in traumatic loss), the effects on the child depend, of course, on personality factors within the child, but importantly on familial and environmental circumstances as well, such as the reactions of other adults to the loss. Does the family talk about it? Does the child end up feeling she is to blame? Does the child feel secure in her attachment to the surviving parent (if there is one)? And, does the loss of one parent mean the emotional loss of the other as well? In Alex's case, following the death of his father, his mother became emotionally unavailable, depressed for long stretches, incapacitated by grief. The death of his father meant abandonment by both parents, and his childhood was inextricably lost forever.

Clients who are avoidant of attachment attempt to emotionally detach themselves from loss. As early as 1937, in an article, "Absence of Grief," Deutsch observed a tendency in some individuals to omit the normal grief reaction usually expected following the loss of a close relationship. She presented four case studies of three middle-aged clients and one young adult, all of whom expressed little or no emotion in relation to losses such as maternal death and parental divorce. Drawing on Deutsch's observations, Bowlby (1980) indicated that self-sufficiency brings with it a tendency to put down sentimentality and to regard tears as a sign of childishness and weakness.

Because strength is seen as a virtue, when losses occur there is a tendency to take pride in behaving as if everything were normal. The client makes attempts to detach herself from feelings of hurt, sadness, sorrow, or other expressions of dependency, isolating herself from friends, particularly when there is a risk that signs of weakness will leak out. The attempt to rush toward normality can be self-defeating. In attempting to convince both herself and others around her that she is coping just fine with an important loss, the individual may engage in behaviors that tell others that exactly the opposite is true.

One client, who began going out on dates just weeks following the death of his wife of 29 years, could not understand why his children "didn't get it." He was doing *fine*; they should stop "making such a fuss" over him and every little decision he was making.

## *Avoidance of Mourning*

In addressing the loss associated with trauma, the importance of mourning cannot be emphasized enough. Mourning is fundamental to the treatment process and critical to bringing about better coping and resolution of acknowledged and unacknowledged emotions. It is a painful and difficult endeavor, but one that is important not to sidestep. Before we consider what is actually mourned during treatment by clients who are avoidant of attachment, it is instructive to think about the ways in which such clients attempt to set aside the mourning process altogether.

### *Minimization*

In Chapter 1, minimization of negative attachment-related experiences was discussed in detail. With respect to the loss associated with trauma, clients tend to avoid the mourning process, using the various minimization strategies discussed previously. All such minimization attempts keep attention focused away from the emotions associated with loss.

Distractions such as excessive involvement in intellectual or instrumental activity, including work or school, often serve to keep painful feelings of loss at bay, as do excessive involvement in leisure-related activities. When attention turns toward emotional aspects of loss, there is a tendency to rationalize events, such that the client considers himself "better off" or "all the stronger for it." The avoidance of mourning is seen quite clearly in families in which there is excessive focus on the legalistic aspects of wills and money. Family members will engage in conflicts, voicing opposing theories on the fair distribution of inheritance monies, often wrangling over details for years, sometimes to the point at which they turn to cutting off the relationship.

---

An elderly woman born in Poland had spent 3 years in hiding during the Holocaust as a young child. Having personally witnessed the killing of both her parents (she had only narrowly escaped), she now sought therapy for help dealing with relentless migraines. She had spent several years ministering to every physical whim and need of her terminally ill husband, who had been incontinent, diabetic, and in need of daily dialysis. Although not the original reason she came for treatment, she was in constant conflict with her daughter, who was running the large grocery business the now-dying father had spent years building. As her husband's condition worsened and as her attachment-related distress heightened, my client and her daughter became increasingly embroiled in conflict related to the will and to money, eventually leading to a cutting off of the relationship for almost a year. Admittedly, this had been her "favorite daughter," whom she now "couldn't stand to look at."

Against a backdrop of a childhood grounded in loss and in the throes of her biggest loss since, my client cut off the one person closest to her. And, during the period when she could have been mourning the death of her husband, she would not return her daughter's phone calls, let her visit, or talk to her, and had enormous difficulty acknowledging any substantive emotional effects due to the loss of her husband.

---

### *Precipitous Forgiveness*

Another way in which such clients tend to avoid mourning is through the use of precipitous forgiveness. On the face of it, forgiveness has much appeal. It seems virtuous, ideal. It demonstrates maturity and the ability to let go. It connotes a position of strength, a rejection of the victim role, and a gesture of return to normalcy (Baumeister, Exline, & Sommer, 1998). After all, to forgive assumes there is a "forgiven," perhaps one who has apologized, communicated remorse, one who has atoned. Forgiveness takes the high road.

However, sometimes forgiveness is used in a way that is emotionally dishonest and not terribly helpful, that is, as a way of avoiding the painful experience of mourning. Herman wrote that some individuals attempt to "bypass their outrage altogether through a fantasy of forgiveness. . . . The survivor imagines that she can transcend her rage and erase the impact of the trauma through a willed, defiant act of love" (1992, p. 189). Among individuals who have difficulty acknowledging feelings of anger, disappointment, and disgust with perpetrators, there is often a rush to forgive.

The problem with precipitous forgiveness is that it fails to account for the real emotional experiences of the client. It cuts out the hurt, sets it aside, instead of integrating it into the individual's life story in an honest, balanced way. And, many clients who are under the impression that they "should" forgive instead feel inadequate when they acknowledge (in moments of honesty with themselves) that they simply cannot bring themselves to do so.

Individuals in this clinical population tend to use precipitous forgiveness as a means of sidestepping emotions that are difficult to address directly. Forgiveness of caregivers who may have knowingly or unwittingly caused traumatic distress is highly compatible with the tendency toward parental idealization. The client may feel pulled toward making excuses on the parent's behalf, forgiving the few faults that are acknowledged at all. As noted, forgiveness is also compatible with the self-image of emotional strength. It allows the individual to avoid feelings of hurt, pain, and vulnerability and instead move directly into a position of socially appropriate strength and grace. The one who grants forgiveness is far more powerful than the one awaiting an apology.

For the therapist, it is tempting to hear the language of forgiveness and to regard the individual with admiration, to see him as mature, strong, impressive. I have sometimes heard students presenting such cases, referring to the client as having a "remarkable attitude." However, it is important not to become unduly drawn in by the client's presentation. Precipitous forgiveness is a means of avoiding losses that continue to have an impact on the individual's life. The therapist's feeling of admiration is one that serves to circumvent the recognition of these deep-seated hurts. Such admiration is a response that the client likely experiences from his other everyday relationships, therefore serving no substantive purpose in psychotherapy other than to provide momentary gratification for the individual and to provide a sense of relief for the therapist, who can be temporarily reassured by the client's "positive attitude."

In contrast, mourning is meaningful, honest, and healing. It comes about through the painful, hard work of acknowledging and experiencing the emotions related to loss, accepting the many complicated, contradictory feelings that accompanied a traumatic history, making sense of the impact such varying emotions have had on the individual's life, and integrating this understanding into the person's view of himself within his relational world. Herman (1992) wrote:

> True forgiveness cannot be granted until the perpetrator has sought and earned it through confession, repentance, and restitution. Genuine contrition in a perpetrator is a rare miracle. Fortunately, the survivor does not need to wait for it. Her healing depends on the discovery of restor-

> ative love in her own life; it does not require that this love be extended to the perpetrator. Once the survivor has mourned the traumatic event, she may be surprised to discover how uninteresting the perpetrator has become to her and how little concern she feels for his fate. She may even feel sorrow and compassion for him, but this disengaged feeling is not the same as forgiveness. (p. 190)

## *What Is There to Mourn?*

### *Early and Recent Losses*

When clients have experienced the physical or emotional loss of a caregiver due to death, divorce, or abandonment during a sensitive period of development or during childhood at large or when clients have experienced the psychological loss of a caregiver due to events surrounding intrafamilial abuse, it is important to encourage discussion of such losses in psychotherapy, particularly discussion that is grounded in the *emotional experience* of the event and its aftermath.

The clinician listens for *affective themes* associated with such losses and invites the individual to clarify, label, and experience different emotions she may have felt both at the time and now, particularly feeling states that the client is not accustomed to considering, such as rejection, sadness, and neediness. In addition, because individuals who avoid attachment tend to idealize one or both caregivers (even those who have been deeply hurtful), it is important that the therapist listen carefully for themes of disappointment in parents as these inevitably surface, but usually in disguised, subtle ways.

Usually, such loss-related affects tend to arise out of context. Because they do, it is easy for the clinician to miss them altogether or to quickly lose the emotional thread, particularly when the individual enthusiastically engages in the tendency to "talk around" (see Chapter 1) attachment-related issues. It is important that the therapist listen for, notice, and bring the client *back to the affect*, not in a mechanistic or pushy way, but in a manner that is true to the moment.

Emotions related to loss, such as rejection, sadness, and neediness are all difficult to own. When they arise, they tend to provoke feelings of dependency and a sense of shame and inadequacy, for example, "I feel stupid for having gotten so upset," and so on. Because they run counter to the client's general self-presentation, emotional themes such as these are difficult to acknowledge, and the individual avoids feeling-oriented questions by responding with thoughts or analytic statements instead or "talks about" feelings instead of experiencing them. Psychologist Leslie Greenberg and colleagues (Greenberg, 2008; Greenberg & Pascual-Leone, 2006) have emphasized the importance of attending to emotional experience when helping clients overcome emotion avoidance, arguing that:

> Emotional awareness is not thinking about feeling, it involves feeling the feeling in awareness. Only when emotion is felt does its articulation in language become an important component of its awareness. The therapist thus needs to help clients approach, tolerate, and accept their emotions. Acceptance of emotional experience as opposed to its avoidance is the first step in emotion work. (Greenberg, 2008, p. 52)

Consistent with this view, when inviting reflection on loss-related experiences, it is often useful to help the client *link feelings to bodily sensations.* McCullough (1998, 2001) emphasized the importance of the bodily experience of affect, particularly when such emotions have not been often talked about or are difficult to put into words. She noted that, in treatment, the feeling should create physiological arousal in the body. "Behavior change does not follow the mere intellectual imaging of affective scenes. The body must be activated for change to occur" (2001, p. 68).

As noted (see Chapter 2), with clients who are avoidant of attachment, there is a disconnection between emotional experience felt in the body and conscious awareness. Recall that in Dozier and Kobak's (1992) study, the authors questioned participants about their attachment-related experiences using the Adult Attachment Interview and found that among the avoidant individuals, there were greater rises in skin conductance, indicating higher levels of anxiety, when discussing attachment-related experiences such as separation, rejection, and threat from parents, despite the fact that the participants consciously denied experiencing distress.

Clinicians focusing particularly on the mind–body connection in trauma (e.g., Ogden, Minton, & Pain, 2006) have observed this disconnection, noting that these clients may appear visibly uncomfortable yet claim to feel fine. Thus, Ogden et al. (2006) emphasized that treatment for these individuals include becoming much more aware of the internal somatic states associated with affective experiences. As the client discusses loss-related experiences, it is helpful to ask what she is feeling just then. What is she experiencing *in her body*? Where is she feeling tension? When does her breathing become faster? Familiar physiological experiences can be easier to access initially than the emotions to which they are connected. For example, Sandra (whose case I detailed in Chapter 1), was willing and able to describe that feeling of her "stomach in knots" in relation to being with her mother both now and in the past, well before she was able to connect such sensations to the feeling of being rejected and hurt by her.

In attempting to link feelings to bodily sensations, it is also useful to *notice discrepancies* between expressed emotions and nonverbal physical behaviors. At times, the disconnection can be striking, with the client's description of loss-related experiences accompanied by an expressed denial of any feelings at all, contrasted with such emotionally laden behaviors as blushing, foot shaking, sitting forward in the chair, perspiration, and so on. But more often, the discrepancy is subtle, and quick recomposure makes it easy for the therapist to miss the moment. For example, a brief cracking of the voice, a single tear, slight reddening of the eyes, crossing or uncrossing of the arms, changes in eye contact, a slight lean forward, and so on all demonstrate nonverbal signs of shifts in affect. In as nonshaming language as possible, it is useful to notice these behaviors and to ask the client what she is *feeling in the moment*. As greater trust develops in the therapeutic relationship, such questions are gradually met with less resistance.

As discussed, the clinician listens for emotional themes associated with trauma-related losses. As such themes arise, it is helpful to link affect to specific "relationship episodes" (Target, Fonagy, & Shmueli-Goetz, 2003), focusing on the feelings associated with specific *autobiographical memories*. Establishing such emotional connections is far more powerful than "talking about" events in a more general intellectualized manner. Instead, it is instructive to ask the client for specific examples of relational situations in which a relevant emotion was experienced. For example, with the self-reliant client, any lifetime experiences of neediness, crying, or sadness are relevant and are important to link to other specific relational situations in which such emotions may have been felt.

In discussing the process of eliciting narratives from clients who are avoidant of attachment, Holmes suggested that the therapist be on the lookout for detailed images, memories, and examples, specific experiences that can help bring perfunctory stories to life. He recommended such questions as "Can you remember an incident that illustrates that?" "When did you start feeling [that way]?" and "Whereabouts in your body do you experience [that feeling]?" (1999, pp. 157–158).

For example, when the client tells an apparently emotionally laden story, referring to an important character by his or her role or title (e.g., "my 'ex,'" "my son," "my doctor," etc.), it is important to ask for the character's name; to get to know the client's stories in a more immediate, *personal* sense; and to encourage the individual to engage in the process of remembering and meaning making without the comfortable distance that comes when referring to people by their roles or titles.

In this process, inviting the client to address loss-related emotions in the context of specific remembered episodes can help with the process of integrating and making sense of such feelings. In so doing, the therapist invites the individual to make meaning of the event or loss and possible effects it may have had on how she views herself and on how she functions within her relational world.

Therapeutic conversations such as this can be experienced initially by the client as odd and uncomfortable and usually would have been inconceivable for the individual to have had at the time the loss took place. As in the case of Alex, the responses of caregivers, and of other important adults, can make a meaningful difference regarding reaction to loss. If the family had always tended toward emotional detachment, then in the face of overwhelming attachment distress, there may be powerful pressure to deactivate attachment-related needs, with expectations not to talk about the event often explicitly imposed by the surviving parent. One client described how following abandonment by her mother when she was a preadolescent, her father transplanted her and her brother to a new residence in South America, taking them from grandparents, friends, school, and home, even going to the point of legally changing all of their first and last names as a way of "starting over." She was never to speak of her mother or mention her name from that point onward, in public or in private.

In cases of intrafamilial sexual or physical abuse, the forced removal of a parent from the home or the imposition of supervised visits (even when these are appropriate from a child protective services standpoint) may be associated with a sense of loss in the child, as well as powerful feelings of ambivalence and guilt because the child may feel ongoing loyalty to the abusive parent, even if the child felt afraid of the parent. In such cases, the response of the nonoffending caregiver can have a strong impact on the way the child negotiates the loss.

The child often experiences a sense of divided loyalty, anger directed toward the nonoffending parent (the only person to whom it is safe enough to direct anger), and the wish that everything would just go back to normal. There is often subtle or direct pressure exerted on the child to voice the view that, for example, "It's much better with Dad gone." Even when true, what tends to go underground is a feeling of sadness about the loss.

When the nonoffending or surviving caregiver is unable to carry out the protective role of parenting in the wake of trauma or traumatic loss, this can have an enormous impact on the child's ability to mourn. For example, if the child is somehow blamed by the surviving parent, it is almost impossible for the child to feel sadness or longing as the feeling of loss is overshadowed by overwhelming feelings of guilt for having "ruined" the family in one way or another. And, when the nonoffending or surviving parent becomes unduly affected by his or her own reaction to traumatic events, this can have an impact on the child's sense that it is safe enough within the relationship to express his own sadness and sorrow. As mentioned, in Alex's case, his mother's overwhelming reaction to the loss of her husband meant the loss of both of his parents, his father due to death and his mother due to the emotional abandonment that took place as she sank deeper into depression.

In helping the client mourn important losses, it is often helpful to use the feelings connected with more recent losses to segue into discussion of earlier ones, that is, to help the individual make emotional *connections* between more *recent losses and earlier ones*. When affective themes arise in stories of difficult current losses, these are noticed, highlighted, and asked about in relation to earlier losses. Interpersonal experiences across the life span are connected largely by the emotions they arouse. In therapy, when emotional themes surface alongside changes in the client's affective or somatic presentation (such as when the individual gets momentarily choked up, demonstrates shifts in nonverbal behavior, and so on), the clinician can take note of such emotional themes and inquire about the individual's history of interpersonal experiences with that feeling.

Contextualizing loss-focused conversations within the here and now (and exploring affective links to earlier losses) makes it much easier for clients who are avoidant of attachment to consider such discussion to be relevant and worthwhile. In time, such a process also helps with the integration of past and present (Cloitre, 2008).

Approximately 4 months into therapy, Alex's mother was diagnosed with an aggressive form of cancer. Although this was the first I heard of it, the illness was apparently not entirely unexpected for Alex. He had known even a couple of months prior to starting therapy that his mother had been going to her doctor for a variety of tests. At the time that I first heard of her illness, I realized that the prospect of losing his mother a second time was likely a factor in his symptomatic decompensation in the first place, several months prior. Initially, it was difficult for him to discuss his feelings about his mother's illness, engaging, in characteristic form, in a host of minimization strategies. Still, the threat of losing her was on his mind and difficult to deactivate entirely.

I would ask Alex about her illness, gently coming back to the topic after his frequent attempts to evade, helping him draw parallels between emotions felt then and now. Over several months in therapy, he would put up fewer and fewer barriers, sometimes even taking initiative to bring in emotional content. And as he was able to engage increasingly in such discussion, we were able to make links to his feelings following his father's death, allowing him to begin mourning in a way he had not done before.

In a particularly poignant moment about a year into treatment, he had been wondering aloud about why he could remember so little of his childhood prior to age 10. Although he could recall the day his father died, he was not sure how much of that was his own memory or what he had been told. Given how bright he was, that fact irritated him. In one session, he recounted a story about his wife and child and what had transpired the night before: At home on the couch, his wife held their infant son on her lap, and as she was leafing through a photo album, pointing out family members to the little one, slowly and deliberately pronouncing their names out loud, it dawned on Alex that it *mattered* to him whether his son knew him, and that he had never before realized how important it was. He did not want his son to have no memory of him the way that he had almost no memory of his own father. For the first time, he had a sense that his father's death was an important, defining moment in his life.

Psychotherapy is not a linear process. And as is often the case, clients "lose" connections gained weeks or even days earlier, only to refind them later along the path. Alex's emotional understanding of his father's death went up and down, deepening over time, both as he felt anxiety and sadness regarding his mother's illness in the here and now and as he mourned other important, related losses associated with his father's death. For clients who are avoidant of attachment, related to the real loss of attachment figures is the loss of the idealized images representing them. In particular, losing the image of having had a "good" or "normal" parent or family is painful and difficult but necessary for growth and development to take place. This was the case for Alex and is discussed next.

### *The Good Parent, the Normal Family*

Coming to the realization that our parents are imperfect and sometimes flawed or limited is a necessary part of normal development. In families in which there is adequate security in the parent–child relationship, there is space for the child to develop balanced, realistic mental representations of her caregivers, so that parental flaws are seen for what they are. With an internalized sense of security comes a certain measure of freedom and flexibility. Seeing the parent's negative characteristics does not mean loss of the relationship and is not experienced as an overwhelming threat.

However, when there is no such security, freedom, and flexibility within the parent–child relationship, it becomes necessary for the child to develop defensive maneuvers to protect her view of one or both parents. As detailed in Chapter 1, parental idealization is an important aspect of avoidant attachment and comes about in a defensive attempt to keep faith in caregivers in the face of genuine parenting inadequacies. In rationalizing harsh, rejecting, punitive, or abusive caregiving, the client may cling to a view of one or both parents as good, normal, or loving.

As the client begins to feel safe within the therapeutic relationship and begins to explore a broader range of feelings surrounding painful life experiences, there is a shift that occurs in her view of her own history, a shift toward seeing caregivers in increasingly balanced terms, with a greater ability to tolerate criticism of parental choices and behaviors, along with a changing characterization of family and childhood. For clients who are avoidant of attachment, such a shift can be frightening and disconcerting. It may come about with feelings of guilt for betraying caregivers and the feeling that one's "normal" family is now lost.

For the therapist, helping the client through this process means taking the loss (of the idealized parental or familial image) seriously; understanding that for the client, experiencing such a change can be destabilizing. It means helping the client examine the painful feelings and the sense of loss that comes with giving up an idealized view of one or both caregivers. It means helping the client face the disorientation that arises in seeing attachment figures through a different lens and the difficulty that comes with having to construct a new familial story when the old one no longer fits.

Still, as the client begins to consider her caregivers and family in different terms, the therapist recognizes that the process is necessary and painful as well as inevitable. It arises in psychotherapy as a consequence of being honest with oneself, out of the experience of feeling increasingly secure within the therapeutic relationship to explore painful aspects of one's life.

In Alex's case, as he became more willing to feel sadness about the loss of his father, a number of changes occurred, particularly in the context of him having recently become a father himself. These included the loss of his perception of having had a normal childhood (up to then, he had always viewed his childhood as normal), a reduction in parental idealization, the realization that his father's excessive drinking likely affected Alex's own tendency toward alcohol and drug abuse and may have even been a factor in the accident that claimed his father's life, and his understanding that, in fact, his mother could have responded better after his father's death. For Alex, one of the hardest feelings to grapple with was his sense of disappointment in both his parents. As a result, one of his biggest practical challenges was in finding a new way to relate to his mother in the here and now as he began to view her in a different light. This was particularly difficult when feelings of guilt and familial disloyalty arose as he thought about her deteriorating condition due to her illness.

## Clinical Overview Points

Things to Remember in Helping Clients with Emotional Detachment

- Value the importance of mourning.
- Pay attention to secondary losses arising from trauma: lost sense of parental protection, loss of childhood, loss of innocence.
- Notice when clients are avoiding mourning, as they use:
  - Minimization

  - Precipitous forgiveness
- Invite the client to look at the emotional experience of the loss and its aftermath, focusing on feeling states such as:
  - Rejection
  - Sadness
  - Neediness
  - Disappointment
- Notice when the emotional thread has been lost in the session, and bring the client back to the affect.
- Help the individual link feelings to bodily sensations.
- Notice discrepancies between expressed emotions and nonverbal physical behaviors.
  - Ask the client what he is feeling in the moment.
- Look at loss-related emotional themes in the context of specific autobiographical memories.
- Get to know the client's experiences in a more immediate, personal sense:
  - Be on the lookout for detailed images, memories, and specific experiences that can bring stories to life.
- Help the individual make emotional connections between more recent losses and earlier ones.
- Explore the loss that comes with giving up an idealized view of caregivers.
  - What difficult feelings go along with a shifting view of one's parents and family?

CHAPTER 5

# Building the Therapeutic Relationship

The therapeutic relationship lies at the heart of any successful therapy. Clinicians across different treatment modalities have noted the centrality of the relationship, viewing it both as a medium of healing in its own right and as a precondition for the successful application of various intervention techniques (Perris, 2000). Navigating the ups and downs of the therapeutic relationship is particularly important with the client who has a history of intrafamilial trauma, whose ongoing relational difficulties are routinely enacted with the therapist, making it challenging to work collaboratively in treatment. Basch viewed the failure to navigate through difficulties in the therapist–client relationship as the most common reason for the failure to move forward in psychotherapy, for the treatment to remain "a boring, circular, repetitive recounting of symptoms, with emphasis on placing the blame for them on external situations" (1980, p. 40).

In this chapter, we turn to the therapeutic relationship, to the roadblocks we face in attempting to connect interpersonally with clients in this population, and to how we may consider addressing such difficulties. How might we navigate the course of this complex relationship, and how might we make use of the relationship in the service of the therapy?

*The Case of Terry*

I started working with Terry, a mother of two in her early 40s, in the aftermath of a sexual assault that had taken place on her eldest son. At the time of the reported offense, it was recommended by the assigned caseworker that both the youth and his mother receive counseling. Terry was given the phone number of her local child treatment agency, but she refrained from calling for approximately 2 months. Subsequently, her son, Christopher, aged 14, started to experience night terrors; a few weeks later, he began sleepwalking, at times reenacting the rape that had occurred in the boys' washroom at school a few months earlier. At that point, Terry followed through with an appointment to have her child assessed. When Christopher began treatment at their local children's mental health center, Terry was referred to me for individual psychotherapy.

Although she made every attempt to put on a brave face, she had difficulty knowing how to cope with the assault. The day after the disclosure, following the multitude of meetings that took place with representatives of the school, law enforcement, and children's aid, she brought her son home, turned on the television, and went to sleep early. For the next few weeks, she would often hear him cry in his bedroom alone, not knowing what to do for him or how to respond to his suffering. On occasion, she would tell Christopher that the older boy who raped him was a terrible person, and that he should "try not to think about it." Sometimes, she would report to him information regarding the ongoing investigation, including the few details that had been shared with her up to that point. Later, when Christopher's therapist asked Terry to take part in some of his treatment sessions, her participation would include complaining about the incompetence of the various professionals involved with the case, staring off into space without saying anything, and at times crying inconsolably.

Despite a cruel and difficult past, Terry had always felt that she had done well for herself. Having worked for years as a hairdresser, she independently supported her family, which included herself and her two children. She noted with pride never having accepted any handouts and never receiving unemployment benefits or help from family members, even at the time that her common-law husband left her when she was 7 months pregnant with Christopher and his fraternal twin sister.

Terry grew up in a home environment best described as critical, distant, and at times frightening. Her father, a commercial airline pilot, would frequently be away. When home, he would ignore Terry unless she did something he disapproved of, which often seemed to revolve around food. He would criticize her when she ate, drawing attention to her weight, referring to her as lazy and irresponsible, and telling her she was acting like a "big baby" when she would cry. During a 9-month period when he was laid off of work, his inability to cope rendered him especially harsh, becoming physically and verbally abusive with both Terry and her mother. Although she struggled with mental illness, Terry's mother tried to physically shield and protect her from the violent rages, once sustaining injuries that included a broken rib.

Nevertheless, her mother's mental illness, a delusional disorder, often incapacitated her, leaving Terry to fend for herself. Worried about her family's money problems, during the sixth grade Terry took an afterschool job stocking shelves at a local grocery store, from which she was fired when caught stealing food items. There were a number of ongoing difficulties that resulted from her mother's delusional disorder. On a few occasions, she barricaded the two of them into the furnace room of their middle-class suburban home, hiding for hours from "the Nazis," "the Warden," and other assumed predators.

It was clear from the beginning of our work that Terry's early traumas were being triggered by the assault on her son. However, consistent with her characteristic way of dealing with attachment-related distress, she would generally sidestep painful emotions, glossing over events by stating, for example, that she "felt bad" for Christopher, but elaborating no further and then crying out of context but unable to say what she was feeling in the moment.

Interpersonally, I found working with Terry to be rather frustrating at first. I sometimes felt as though we were at cross purposes; we were not connecting in the way I normally did with my clients. During the initial sessions, she maintained a somewhat practical stance, focusing on issues related to the ongoing investigation, Christopher's sporadic school attendance, and some behavioral problems that had developed for Christopher's twin sister. Although these sessions did seem helpful to her in an instrumental way, it also felt as though our discussions were all too controlled and censored.

My own children were quite young at the time, and during sessions, I often found that Christopher's rape would be on my mind. I could not help but imagine myself as the parent in this scenario, a parent feeling helpless, guilty, and inept. Yet, I could say little to Terry that seemed like it hit the mark, particularly when I would inquire about her relationship with Christopher. At times, it felt as if I were digging in the wrong spot, as though there was nothing there. At other times, when she would cry "for no reason" (her words), she would look at me with what appeared to be disdain, accusing me of unnerving her.

Ironically, the moments in the therapy that were particularly difficult to navigate were those when I felt we had formed some kind of brief, empathic connection. Fleeting as they were, it seemed that as soon as a chord had been touched, Terry would pull away, would quickly discount the interaction, or would become anxious, questioning aloud whether she should be in therapy at all. With Terry, it felt as though the normal tools of the trade were invariably doomed to fail, and my attempts at empathy and at forming a meaningful, therapeutic connection would inevitably backfire.

---

## Connection, Vulnerability, and the Distancing Maneuver

It is difficult to put into words or to define operationally what exactly goes into the formation of the interpersonal connection that develops between therapist and client. Yet, as mentioned in Chapter 2, studies using meta-analysis (e.g., Wampold, 2001), which summarize findings across numerous investigations, and draw on various treatment models, have found the therapeutic relationship to be a critical factor for successful outcome in psychotherapy.

### *Forming a Therapeutic Connection: Empathy*

Attachment theory places considerable emphasis on the importance of the therapeutic relationship. Sable (2000) stated that within the interpersonal space between self and other, an interaction takes place between two individuals marked by emotional contact and understanding. Sable went on to say that when the therapist becomes a secure base for the client, she promotes a sense of safety for exploration, making it is possible for the client to experience a healing, reparative relationship that is internalized. Many others (e.g., Aron, 1996) have also underscored the importance of the interpersonal space between self and other in therapy, often emphasizing empathy and the emotional nature of the therapeutic encounter.

Bowlby (1988) maintained that there is no information more vital for reconstructing working models of self and other than information about how therapist and client feel toward the other:

> During the earliest years of our lives, indeed, emotional expression and its reception are the only means of communication we have, so that the foundations of our working models of self and attachment figure are perforce laid using information from that source alone. Small wonder therefore, if, in reviewing his attachment relationships during the course of psychotherapy and restructuring his working models, it is the emotional communications between a patient and his therapist that play the crucial part. (p. 157)

Such connection is fostered through a climate of reliability, attentiveness, and emotional responsiveness. "The therapist strives . . . to see and feel the world through his patient's eyes, namely to be empathic" (Bowlby, 1988, p. 140). In his classic text on psychotherapy, Havens (1986) examined the therapeutic relationship and the language of empathy in detail, arguing that with clients who have figuratively "hidden themselves away," either for protection or in response to their own or others' criticisms, the therapist "finds the other" by engaging in an exploration of the other's world, by imagining the experience of the other and then expressing it. Havens emphasized the importance of active forms of empathy, describing the process of attuning oneself closely to what the client may have felt and then translating these emotions into words, contending that empathy is the clinical equivalent of intimacy: "The most certain way of knowing when a person is present, of finding the other, lies in the ability to empathize with that person" (1986, p. 16).

In describing the challenge of forming a therapeutic connection with individuals who are avoidant of attachment, Holmes (1997) similarly stressed the need to establish some kind of empathic, emotional connection early in the work. Using language reminiscent of Havens' (1986) term *making contact*, Holmes suggested that with such clients, one of the first tasks of treatment is to establish "emotional contact," often, in his view, through tears or anger, and that any evidence of real intimacy must be reinforced and welcomed. Consistent with the attachment theorists described, Holmes considered such intimacy to be the recognition that "therapist and patient have separate yet shared mental space" (1997, p. 242).

The value of empathy and the importance of emotional connection within the developing therapeutic relationship were underscored by Liotti (2007). He proposed that in working with the avoidant client, the therapist show "immediate, explicitly empathic attitudes" to the individual's description or expression of painful emotions. He went on to say that:

> Therapists should take pains over showing to the patients that expressing attachment emotions (i.e., fear, pain, discomfort, loneliness, sadness for losses, wish for comfort, joy at reunions after separations, etc.) is welcome, normal to being a human being, not shameful and not annoying to the therapist in the least. In other words, therapists should help patients re-code these feelings or felt needs from being threatening to being safe to share and explore (p. 149).

### *How Feelings of Vulnerability Arise*

Empathy can be destabilizing. When the therapist reacts in a manner that runs counter to the client's prior experiences with caregivers and a meaningful connection comes about, this can in fact create a variety of uncomfortable mixed feelings. The client who has received so little attunement, so little understanding, may not know what to make of such interactions. Can the therapist be trusted? Will he inevitably respond in the same hurtful way that others have? Pearlman and Courtois (2005) wrote that in the more severe cases of trauma, the therapist's very reliability and consistency "may be incomprehensible and threatening (p. 454)."

Feeling understood means being seen, having one's suffering witnessed, but it also means being exposed. It happens when the client momentarily lets down her guard, when the individual opens herself to a new interpersonal connection, but it comes at a price. It comes with the risk of further loss and pain. In short, empathy means vulnerability. And, while vulnerability is a necessary condition for the development of intimacy in any relationship, for clients in this population it gives rise to an uneasy sense that they are no longer fully protected.

When discomfort arises out of an empathic connection, it does so because some unbearable fear has been provoked. Feeling vulnerable within the therapeutic relationship is a frightening experience. Attachment theory suggests that with clients who are avoidant of attachment, the developing connection with the therapist provokes fears of closeness and dependency (Wallin, 2007) and therefore the potential for rejection, loss, and the reemergence of the hurt and pain that went along with prior experiences.

By empathizing with the client, the therapist is asking for a lot. He is asking that the individual go against prior experience and take a leap of faith that this time things will be different. This time, her vulnerability will give rise to a sensitive, responsive relationship. But, on what basis should she take such a leap of faith? Common sense tells her not to, and fear pulls her back.

As described, a developing empathic connection with the therapist provokes a sense of vulnerability. For clients in this population, an additional aspect of this vulnerability is related to feelings of humiliation and a sense of judgment (Mallinckrodt et al., 2005). Experiences of caregiver criticism and rejection early in life can make for a heightened sense of personal responsibility and self-reliance as well as a strong tendency to judge oneself harshly, especially following moments of personal weakness. In Terry's case, I would often observe this in the aftermath of a particularly compelling moment in the therapy. She would often respond with self-criticism if she showed what could be construed as a sign of weakness, sometimes chastising herself for what she had expressed to me. At the end of one session, after the next appointment had been scheduled, on exiting the room, she commented on having promised herself that week that she was not going to cry in session. The following meeting, when I asked her about her previous week's comment, after some discussion she confessed that therapy was "one of the hardest things I've ever had to do."

### *The Distancing Maneuver: Back to Self-Protection*

A state of vulnerability cannot be sustained for long. It feels unsafe and disconcerting. A sense of instability has been triggered, and the client becomes motivated to restore the control that comes with self-protection. The *distancing maneuver* does just that. It restores equilibrium to a relationship that has started to feel a little too close for comfort.

When emotional vulnerabilities arise in the therapeutic relationship, the client backs away. As a form of transference, the distancing maneuver represents both the avoidance of the developing relationship with the therapist and the avoidance of the attachment-related feelings the relationship provokes. In restoring interpersonal distance between therapist and client, it offers temporary relief for the individual who does not know what to make of his feelings of closeness and dependency, and it allows the client again to disavow (Steiner, 1993) the whole idea of being understood by an important other.

A number of attachment theorists have described the process of client vulnerability followed by such acts of distancing. Mary Connors' (1997) article on avoidant attachment in psychotherapy indicated that:

> The notion of relying on a new attachment figure will be strenuously resisted by those who have been consistently rebuffed and treated harshly in the original attachment relationship. . . . Inquiries into emotional states will be puzzling and foreign to patients whose caregivers discouraged expression of negative affects, and may signal potential retraumatization. (p. 485)

Connors went on to state that the therapist should expect withdrawal from these individuals, such that moments of vulnerability would be followed by renewed defensiveness.

The distancing maneuver has been illustrated in a few case studies reported in the clinical literature. Both Slade (2004) and Liotti (2002) described cases of adult women (with backgrounds similar to those of clients presented here) whose tendencies were to pull back from the therapeutic relationship, particularly when vulnerabilities were provoked. Slade understood this as the client managing the therapeutic relationship, and its intrinsic demands for closeness and reflection, and in the process reenacting experiences of separation, abandonment, and loss. Similarly, Liotti explained his client's distancing behaviors in terms of attachment-related processes, stating that:

> As soon as she started feeling attached to the therapist (which was shown by her emotional involvement in the therapeutic dialogue . . . ), the interpersonal schema related to her original avoidance of the attachment figure was activated, and she felt almost compelled to avoid meeting the therapist. (p. 380)

Empirical investigations have found results consistent with the observations reported in the clinical literature. Although they have not looked at the specific process by which avoidant clients retreat from empathic connections with the therapist, they have corroborated the general idea that such individuals do struggle with closeness within the relationship (Daniel, 2006), and that they tend to put psychological distance between themselves and the clinician. In a study of adults in brief therapy, Mallinckrodt et al. (2005) found that clients who were avoidant of attachment were more likely to be reluctant to self-disclose and to have difficulty trusting the therapist. Similarly, an investigation looking at the therapeutic relationship among avoidant clients with trauma histories specifically (Kanninen et al., 2000) found the ending of therapy to be particularly difficult on the therapeutic alliance; the authors explained that clients coped with the impending separation by distancing themselves from their therapists.

Interestingly, experimental studies in social psychology have reported complementary findings. When individuals avoidant of attachment were placed in circumstances that ostensibly provoked feelings of closeness, acceptance, or reminders of past intimacy, they responded to individuals with whom they had been partnered for various tasks by distancing themselves from those others, becoming disparaging (Bartz & Lydon, 2006), unsympathetic (Haji, McGregor, & Kocalar, 2005), or even aggressive (Logue, 2006). These results demonstrate the difficulties encountered when such individuals come up against multiple threats associated with interpersonal closeness.

## Addressing Connection, Vulnerability, and the Distancing Maneuver Within the Therapy Relationship Itself

So, what can be done? How do you reach the person who is uncertain about wanting to be reached? For the therapist, it is especially difficult to see that whenever the client lets down his guard, rather than feeling unburdened, he feels exposed, foolish, and awkward. As a therapist, this is hard to take. It makes the clinician want to back off and return to less-threatening issues, and it may be tempting to do just that, to shy away and relate on a more intellectualized level, to stick more closely to comfortable topics.

Certainly with individuals who have traumatic histories, gentleness is a virtue. I do find it important to ease the client into painful topics, working at a pace his anxieties can bear, not coming on too strongly at first, not overwhelming him. In discussing the challenging task of establishing a therapeutic alliance with untrusting clients, Connors (1997) suggested that early in therapy the clinician engage the individual's intellectual interests and curiosities, particularly if the discussion can incorporate terms, references, and analogies that relate to the person's areas of interest and expertise. A process of easing the client in can give him some space to become socialized into what is an entirely new interaction, and that is helpful, especially early in treatment.

Still, there is only so far this will go. As discussed in previous chapters, sidestepping discussion of traumatic experiences and related emotions does not work in the long run. If the therapist is attuned, asks the painful attachment-related questions, listens nonjudgmentally, and expresses an understanding of the client's experience, over time a therapeutic connection will develop, a connection that is critical to the process of recovery. But, it is this very connection that is so difficult for such clients to tolerate, and the individual will find a way to retreat (Steiner, 1993), distancing himself in one way or another.

For the clinician, the trick is to resist the temptation to retreat as well. Instead, the therapist attempts to make sense of the *process occurring between them*; to understand their moments of connection, vulnerability, and the self-protective distancing that follows; to highlight the ways in which attachment and separation are negotiated in the space between therapist and client. Using the therapeutic relationship in this way provides a here-and-now opportunity to challenge old patterns of intimacy and to rework models of self and other.

### *Using the Distancing Maneuver: A Therapeutic Opportunity*

If we are to help our clients understand the ways in which they put distance between themselves and others, we have to be able to address the process when it occurs with us. However, doing so is easier said than done.

Using the distancing maneuver as a therapeutic opportunity is difficult to do in practice. When the client brings distance into the psychotherapy relationship, he does so as a means of coping with his vulnerabilities. But in the moment, it may be hard for us to experience it that way. One reason is that when they occur, distancing maneuvers often trigger our personal insecurities.

This makes it difficult to see such client behaviors for what they are. Instead, we become caught up in our own feelings in the moment. It is not so easy to maintain composure and therapeutic neutrality in relation to a client who has just pushed you away.

There are so many ways the individual can create distance between himself and the therapist, and each provokes different feelings depending on the clinician's own personal history and the strength of the therapeutic relationship. The client may discount or dismiss therapist comments, may continuously "forget to mention" critical ongoing attachment-related events, may come across as arrogant or superior, and may "forget about" therapy sessions altogether. At the moment that they occur, each of these will trigger feelings in the clinician: rejection, hurt, irritation, anxiety, and so on. And, instead of having the presence of mind to help the individual reflect on underlying motivations for his behavior, the therapist may get caught up in an enactment, reacting to some difficult, painful feeling or vulnerability triggered in her.

Many years ago, I worked with a client who was in the process of completing his second year of study in law. A mature student a few years older than me, he had grown up in a violent home, where he learned to lay low to avoid getting into trouble. Although his parents disdainfully referred to those with higher education as "eggheads," my client spoke with an air of sophistication and a vocabulary that undoubtedly set him apart from just about everyone he encountered. In sessions with him, I would often find myself feeling agitated, trying too hard, trying to sound smart. More often than not, my comments would fall flat or would be ignored altogether, leaving me feeling deflated and incompetent.

I realized my own feelings were likely getting in the way when, one afternoon, I caught myself thumbing uneasily through a dictionary looking up the meanings of at least three words he had used that morning in session. But, it was in clinical supervision that I made an important connection. It had been just a couple of years since I made the decision to pursue a career in psychology rather than law. And to some extent, the decision still felt unresolved, in part because of what I had imagined a career in law would have meant to my own family. Not being able to see past my own feelings, I had let myself get drawn into a competitive enactment, so that when the client put on airs of superiority, I had difficulty seeing these for what they were: a means of compensating for the affection and confidence he otherwise lacked as well as a means of both differentiating himself from and putting himself above a family that had caused him such pain.

Another reason distancing maneuvers are hard to see as therapeutic opportunities is that they occur within a relationship that already feels a bit shaky. When a relationship feels tenuous, one is motivated to make as few waves as possible, that is, to avoid change.

Let us think back to the context in which the distancing maneuver takes place. The clinician is working with an individual who has had painful traumatic experiences but who has rarely, if ever, discussed them with anyone. The therapist is mindful that building trust with this person will likely be a slow, arduous process. As the therapeutic relationship develops, as the client begins to express attachment-related emotions and the clinician expresses empathy, the individual begins to feel exposed, vulnerable, and he responds by pulling back, perhaps by coming to the next session saying that because things are now a lot better, this will be his last appointment. Or, he announces that because he did most of the talking last week, it is better if you did all the talking this week. Perhaps the client now minimizes an important issue that just a week earlier he seemed bothered by, or instead of sticking with the difficult issue, he complains that therapy is not making anything better at all.

In the developing relationship between therapist and client, things now feel tenuous. There is a sense of conflict in the relationship and the possibility that the conflict might be unmanageable; the relationship might even be in jeopardy. In response to empathy, understanding, and warmth, the client has recently started to *feel something* toward the therapist: closeness, annoyance at being made to feel complicated emotions, anxiety about having shared a secret. And, the therapist has also started to feel something toward the client: encouraged that a meaningful connection may be starting to develop, fear that she may have pushed the client too hard, uncertainty about where to go from here. The mixed feelings arising from a sense of closeness make this a tenuous point in the relationship.

When arriving at the point at which the client's feelings of vulnerability have led to some type of distancing process, the therapist has a choice. She can decide to back off and spend the next few sessions dealing with less-threatening topics. In fact, this may need to happen for a while. Perhaps the relationship has been moving forward a bit too quickly; emotions have been coming out too intensely to bear. The therapist may need to observe the closeness/distancing pattern a few more times to feel confident that it is, indeed, a pattern.

But at some point, the clinician will need to *address the pattern of distancing* within the relationship. Whenever that happens, whether weeks or months into the relationship, it will feel stressful. The therapist, suspecting a high likelihood of her observations being rejected or dismissed, will feel vulnerable, unsure of where this will go. But if she can recognize such feelings, and not let them get in the way, there is an enormous opportunity here.

Examining cycles of closeness and distance between therapist and client means putting the relationship right under the spotlight and asking: What is happening right here, right now, between us? The therapist may ask the client directly: What was the hardest part about crying in front of me? What was scary about telling me that? How does it feel now talking about this with me?

Looking at relational processes occurring within the therapy creates the potential for the clinician to feel rejected, hurt, and dismissed, but it also has the potential to lay the foundations for intimacy: for the client to experience his feelings as acceptable to another; for the client to experience the willingness of an important other to be vulnerable; and for the client to experience emotional vulnerability as something that brings strength, not weakness. Thus, the therapeutic relationship can present an opportunity for the individual to learn to make sense of his feelings of vulnerability. In this manner, the relationship can become an instrument for the development of intimacy and can help clarify for the client why so many relationships in his past have felt so tortured.

### *Addressing the Feelings That Go Along With Closeness and Distancing*

There are various ways to bring the interpersonal process to the client's attention, and some are more effective than others. Within this clinical population, as with any group, there are important individual differences, such that some clients are more or less defensive, some therapists and clients are better suited to one another, and some interventions that hit home once an alliance has developed may not have worked so well earlier in the process. When the clinician sees the treatment opportunity and is considering turning the client's attention toward the therapeutic relationship itself, it is always hard to predict how any one individual will respond.

One way of addressing the therapeutic relationship is by adopting a direct explanatory approach. That is, commenting or observing aloud on the process that seems to be going on in the relationship (e.g., "I wonder if you might be feeling that way toward me because I remind you of . . . ?" or "Of course you pull away from everyone; it's what you've had to do to survive . . . ."). In my experience, with many clients, and particularly with this population, such an approach tends to have only mixed success. Its usefulness primarily turns on the extent to which the therapeutic alliance has had time to develop, that is, if client and therapist together have successfully negotiated other, goal-directed interactions, or if there has been some history in the therapeutic relationship of the client accepting attachment-related ideas in other, less-threatening, contexts.

Unfortunately, much of the time I have experienced the direct explanatory approach to be only partially effective, especially when used as a stand-alone intervention. Even when couched in an interpretive statement that grounds psychological causes in current or past relationships, direct explanatory comments, on their own, often fall flat. At best, the client gives her perfunctory agreement, with the therapist unsure of where to go from there. Or, the client may agree in a fleeting or intellectualized way without *feeling* the true impact that such closeness/distancing processes actually have on her life. So, even if the client accepts the idea in principle, it lacks teeth; the emotional thrust is missing.

### *Addressing Feelings of Vulnerability in the Moment*

Instead of adopting a direct explanatory approach, which often keeps things at an intellectualized level, it is more effective to help the client gain an *emotional* understanding of her interpersonal patterns within the therapeutic relationship. The therapist, attending to closeness/distancing patterns as they unfold in the relationship, turns the client's attention toward felt experience, asking the individual to reflect on what she may be *feeling in the moment* and what her feelings may mean. Within the client–therapist relationship, instances of vulnerability as well as acts of distancing can be used productively in the service of the therapy when they are connected in a more immediate sense to client emotional experience.

Let us look at this further. As discussed, a sense of vulnerability often arises in the context of an empathic connection when the individual momentarily lets down her guard. The client's voice may begin to crack; she may shift uncomfortably, briefly avert her eyes, pause as if to recompose herself, criticize herself for getting visibly upset, and so on. At that point, when the therapist observes what seem to be signs of client vulnerability, it is useful to ask, gently but directly, what she is feeling right then. When the client responds (as is often the case) with a thought rather than a feeling, the clinician is accepting, but then encourages her to unpack it further. For example, "You said you're feeling 'like a silly schoolgirl in the principal's office.' As you have that thought, what are you feeling?" Or "What does it feel like, discussing this with me?" Or "What is the hardest part about discussing this with me?" It is often helpful to probe further with, "As we talk about this, what are you feeling in your body right now?"

Following such discussion, it is important to watch for what the client does and says just afterward, for the therapist to note his own feelings, and to take a pulse on the therapeutic relationship. What unfolded, and how did the session end? The therapist may breathe a sigh of relief if the session ended collaboratively ("Finally, . . . we're making some progress . . . ."). But for the client who tries so hard to appear strong, it is difficult to lose control in therapy. In the days to follow, she may feel increasingly exposed and may become quite anxious about the next session.

### *Addressing Feelings Associated With Distancing Maneuvers*

As presented, the distancing maneuver is an indirect expression of discomfort with closeness. It is useful in that it provides the clinician with the opportunity to observe the individual's difficulties with intimacy in the context of the therapeutic relationship. Thus, for the therapist, the distancing maneuver can function as a communication, as a signal that some important vulnerability has been triggered, but one the client is loath to express openly.

The clinician who notices such behavior and registers it as an act of distancing can reflect on it and ask himself what interpersonal process is taking place. What may account for the client pulling away? What painful issue might the individual be avoiding? What anxiety or fear is closeness provoking? What other painful emotions are surfacing?

When the therapist notices distancing and considers the possibility that the client may be momentarily pulling back from the therapeutic relationship, he can address the process on the affective level, turning the client's attention toward the *feelings that go along with* the distancing. Here also, it is important to address the feelings in the moment or as close to the moment as possible. As acts of distancing arise, the clinician asks the individual what she may be feeling right then, what it is like to feel this way, and what she is feeling toward the therapist.

Addressing the feelings that go along with distancing maneuvers requires the therapist to notice and turn the client's attention to those moments in which relevant *emotional shifts* occur. This means both noticing emotional shifts as they take place, within and across sessions, and working with the client to make sense of them. The therapist may notice behaviors that are geared toward *covering up,* keeping feelings from the therapist that would be unflattering or socially unacceptable. For example, as the therapist inquires about the decision to have an affair, the client's body language closes down, indicating a reluctance to discuss it further. Or, the therapist may notice behaviors oriented toward *taking back* prior expressions of emotion (e.g., "You're now telling me you're 'fine,' but a minute ago you didn't look so fine. What happened just there?"). Or, the therapist may notice behaviors that are *reactions to* emotions previously expressed. For example, after expressing sadness over the recent loss of a pet, the client criticizes herself for having looked so foolish in front of the therapist or criticizes the therapist for "making" her talk about upsetting things all the time.

In each of these cases, the therapist can notice and turn the client's attention to those moments in which the relevant emotional shift occurred and can help the client address her feelings as they are experienced. For example, consider the client who criticizes the therapist or the therapy for not helping her after she had just expressed something personal. The therapist, unruffled by the provocation, can hold the moment right there, asking the client to look at the interaction between them and to consider her feelings toward the therapist. What is difficult about revealing that personal detail? What fears or anxieties does it raise? What feels risky about trusting the therapist like that? This process is most useful if the therapeutic alliance has developed over some time and if there is a gradual bringing in of emotional and attachment-related themes throughout the course of the therapy.

As emotions are expressed in the immediate context of the psychotherapy relationship, these can be connected to patterns occurring in other current or past relationships. When dramas related to closeness/distancing unfold in the here and now of the psychotherapy relationship, they carry an immediacy that can be used to build a meaningful understanding of processes that unfold across the client's everyday life. In this way, patterns of intimacy can be illuminating when they are meaningfully connected across life contexts by emotional experience. In time, the client can come to appreciate how the feelings underlying these patterns are a motivating force in her relational behavior.

---

Let's think back to the case of Terry, described at the beginning of this chapter. Recall that she struggled tremendously with her son Christopher's dependency needs after he was raped at his school, often trying to talk him out of his distress, but instead upsetting him further. Most of her relationships with men had ended up in some kind of abandonment, with her husband having left her when she was 7 months pregnant with twins, as well as her father having emotionally abandoned her when she was very young and becoming physically abusive with both her and her mother. Recall also how difficult it was for Terry to be in a position of receiving empathy, how she would pull away when a chord had been touched.

Approximately 6 months after we began working together, I found out that Terry had lost her job. She had been working for years as a hairdresser. Although she had been notified months earlier that the salon was scheduled to close, she did not inform me until she had already been out of work for several months. In other words, at some point in the process, I realized that in addition to coping with a child who had recently been sexually assaulted, she had also gone through the process of being informed that she would lose her job, losing it, and then going on unemployment benefits without mentioning anything to me about it. That is to say, she went though it all alone.

Despite being in weekly therapy, she was reluctant to use me for support, reluctant to use the relationship available to her. Later, I would learn that throughout that time she had, in fact, told no one: not her sister, not her children, no one. And, because the secret leaked out in session (an inadvertent expression of connection to me), I was now the only one who knew.

She said little, but nodded tearfully, when I noted how difficult it must have been for her to go through something like that all alone. And when I asked what it meant to her that I now knew this personal secret, she shifted uncomfortably in her chair, looking a bit frightened. After a couple of passes at the question, she acknowledged that it felt a bit weird and awkward.

She did not show up to the next session, then called the following day to reschedule. When we next met, I revisited the issue when she mentioned that she had declined receiving the free help she was legally entitled to in the job search process. She reasoned that as long as I was the *only* one who knew, then maybe it was not so bad, but if anyone else were to find out, that could become a Pandora's box. I asked her what she felt when she imagined her secret getting out. The words that came to her were "out of control" and "embarrassing."

I pointed out how long she had waited to tell me, how she seemed uncomfortable about my knowing, and I wondered what she may have been *feeling toward me* all that time that she held her secret inside. She responded that she knew I would not "yell at her," but that she felt "embarrassed" and "afraid" to tell me about it, as well as "foolish" for losing her job. She worried that I would think her weak and incapable of finding new employment.

Later in the session, as we discussed further what it meant to her that I knew this secret about her, she told me that, in fact, there were a number of things she had spoken with me about that she had never shared with anyone else, and that she found that a bit "scary." In fact, she found trusting me altogether scary. For example, when she was away on vacation at one point earlier in the year, she found herself wondering what I would think of a couple of the places she had visited, and that made her worry that perhaps she was coming to therapy too much. I reflected to her on how frightening it is for her to depend on me as well as important others, and we discussed some of the mixed feelings that get triggered for her when she does.

She cancelled the following session but again called to reschedule. When we next met, I inquired about her recent pattern of cancelling/rescheduling and what she thought it might mean. After initially ducking the question, she considered that it might be her way of wanting to "not deal with" psychotherapy for a week, which I then encouraged her to reflect on further. Over the next few sessions, we began discussing other secrets in her family: How she could not tell anyone about the physical abuse for years because if she had, her father's own job loss at the time (which was a family secret) would have leaked out, and she was sworn to secrecy, and how her family's many secrets meant she was often uncomfortable bringing her friends home.

---

As mentioned, it is also important for the therapist to help the client use expressed feelings to connect to other thematically related experiences. When relevant emotions come up in the context of the psychotherapy relationship, these can be connected to patterns occurring in other current or past relationships. It is instructive to draw on the emotional language of the client, to consider the emotional words that the individual herself has expressed, and to use these as *points of entry* to get at other important, thematically related experiences.

So with Terry, I would ask about her experience with embarrassment, her experience with fear, and the roles that embarrassment and fear have each played in her life. In this way, we began to look at *other specific moments* of embarrassment and fear in her life, like how she was embarrassed by her mother's mental illness and often afraid of her father, and how more recently she felt too embarrassed to tell her friends about Christopher's rape, so she tried to keep it a secret but ultimately could not.

Once the therapeutic relationship has begun to open up, once there has been some direct expression of emotion within the relationship and a making sense of such expression, at that point the individual has experienced an interaction that has been colored by attachment-related affect. This likely represents a unique experience for the client, so it is helpful to *debrief*.

The clinician can ask about what it was like for the client to have had such an interaction. What part was most or least difficult? How was this interaction similar to or different from those the individual has had with others? What effect has it had on her feelings toward the therapist and the therapy? It is important not to presuppose what this might have been like for the client, but rather to use this as an opportunity to encourage the individual to reflect on emotions she experienced, to help her ultimately feel less threatened by processes that trigger attachment-related affect. It is not unusual for discussions that center on the therapeutic relationship (even when such discussions go well) to feel a bit frightening, to raise further vulnerabilities. After all, there is always the possibility that the therapist's good intentions may or may not be worthy of the client's limited trust.

## Clinical Overview Points

Things to Remember in Building the Therapeutic Relationship

- Value the use of empathy.
- Attempt to make emotional contact from early in treatment.
- Recognize that empathy provokes client vulnerabilities:

  - Anxiety about trusting the therapist, fear of dependency
  - Self-criticism, self-judgment, fear of being or appearing weak
- Notice subtle expressions of vulnerability:
  - Look for verbal and nonverbal signs.
  - Address such sentiments in the moment.
  - Watch for emotional aftereffects.
- Be on the lookout for distancing maneuvers.
- Consider the distancing maneuver to be:
  - An act of self-protection
  - A therapeutic opportunity
- Recognize that addressing closeness or distancing in the relationship can be stressful on the therapist.
- Be aware of what distancing maneuvers tend to provoke in you:
  - Feelings of rejection, hurt, irritation, anxiety, and so on
  - The tendency to back off, to keep things as they are
- Listen for and address feelings that go along with distancing maneuvers:
  - Notice emotional shifts in relation to the therapist.
  - Address such feelings and shifts in the moment.
    - As acts of distancing arise, what was the client feeling toward you?
  - Use such feelings as points of entry, helping connect emotions expressed in the therapy relationship to patterns occurring in other current or past relationships.
    - Look at other specific moments in which the relevant emotion has come up in the client's life.
  - Remember to debrief: What was it like to talk about the therapeutic relationship in this way?

CHAPTER 6

# Understanding Countertransference

A couple of years ago, prompted by my upcoming high school reunion, I had the opportunity to have lunch with a childhood friend from my old neighborhood. Having both grown up in the same Toronto suburb, part of the same circle of friends at the time, we had a lot of catching up to do. During our get-together, somewhere between comparing child-rearing notes and recounting school anecdotes, we got on the topic of psychotherapy.

He knew from years earlier that I had become a psychologist, and although he was a far cry from "psychologically minded," his recent divorce led him to seek treatment, sparking a colorful conversation about his ex-wife, the purpose of therapy in general, and the impression he had of his therapist in particular. Having worked for years in the field of finance, he found the whole enterprise of psychotherapy rather intriguing and was perhaps a little enamored with it. In fact, I suspected that he was possibly imagining a career change for himself as he presented me with a few questions suggesting as much.

As we continued our discussion, my old friend, curious about psychotherapists, asked me a pointed question that got me thinking: "What's in it for *you*?" he inquired. Given how invested he seemed to be in his treatment, and the connection he seemed to have with his therapist, I suspected that he had a fairly good idea even before asking. Still, it was a fair question, and in the moment, I was not all that clear on the answer.

As we embark on working with difficult clients, we have to honestly ask ourselves what *is* in it for us. This is particularly relevant when working with individuals with histories of trauma, who by and large represent the most challenging of cases. In my experience, therapists who specialize in the treatment of traumatized adults vary widely in regard to personal motivation for the work. On a more basic level, they are almost always accepting, compassionate people motivated in part by a wish to help those in need. However, the helping role is often multifaceted, with obvious and subtle motivating forces, including, for example, that aspect of helping that is closely tied to *rescuing* others in need, along with the personal gratification that rescuing brings. Pearlman and Courtois proposed that with many clinicians who work in the area, there is often a tendency to try to rescue or even reparent clients in an attempt to help them make up for what they "deserved but did not receive in childhood" (2005, p. 455), sometimes leading to an overgiving that is marked by exhaustion and resentment on the part of the therapist.

For the client who is being helped (or rescued), the therapist's attention and concern may be received with strong feelings of ambivalence. As described throughout this book, individuals in this clinical population struggle with the very idea of being helped, of needing and depending on the therapist, and they often engage in a variety of help-rejecting, defensive maneuvers oriented toward distancing themselves from the clinician as well as important others. In a classic paper on the therapeutic relationship and the therapist's stance with hard-to-treat clients, Winnicott (1969/1971) emphasized the importance of the client's *use* of the therapist and the therapy, noting that some individuals struggle tremendously with how to engage in treatment and do not know how to make use of the relationships available to them.

In previous chapters, we discussed a number of strategies to engage such clients more actively. In this chapter, we look at the effects *on the therapist* of having a client who does not quite know how to use her, a client who responds to threatening and complicated feelings by dismissing or discounting clinician comments, criticizing himself for having painful feelings to begin with or putting down the enterprise of psychotherapy altogether. How do such client responses affect the therapist and the therapeutic relationship? What role does the clinician play in the process? How do therapist motivations affect the treatment? This chapter looks at some of the problematic ways the therapist may act on the personal feelings that are provoked through the course of therapy.

When the therapist is not used, she is liable to feel unimportant, dispensable. She may even feel rejected, as the client often behaves in a rejecting manner, projecting outward those feelings that are just too difficult to keep inside. In working with this clinical population, it is not possible to escape feelings of rejection, hurt, a sense of incompetence, self-doubt, and anxiety. Individuals who have histories of rejection often provoke feelings of rejection in others. This in part is why so many children of individuals who are avoidant of attachment tend to manifest attachment insecurity themselves. Interpersonal acts of self-protection such as distancing and help-rejecting behavior as well as fear of dependency tend to convey a message to others that they are not needed. This is hard on the therapist, who is drawn toward the helping role, who values being needed, being relied on, feeling like she is making a difference in the life of another.

As therapists, the feelings that get provoked in us are useful. They can be a signal that something frightening or threatening is getting triggered for the client but is too difficult for him to tolerate, or that something that the client said was particularly painful for us because of our own histories or vulnerabilities. The therapist must work *to recognize* such feelings when they occur and to use them in the service of the therapy, to notice them, and to view their presence as an opportunity to reflect on what might have been triggered for the client.

Importantly, difficulties arise not because of the *feelings* that get provoked in the clinician. Rather, when difficulties arise, it is because the therapist has *acted on* those feelings; she has acted on her countertransference. There are many ways that this occurs, and all such patterns represent attempts at coping with feelings that are difficult to bear. For example, in Chapter 2, when we looked at the complexities inherent in challenging avoidant defenses, we noted the difficulties that arise when the therapist either overchallenges or underchallenges the client. In the former, out of feelings of frustration with client defensiveness, the clinician becomes overly keen and aggressive and in the process overchallenges the individual. In the latter, the therapist is pulled in the direction of "not imposing," not wishing to further the client's pain, and in the process underchallenges. As suggested in Chapter 2, there is a fine line to walk between these two alternatives. The ability to find that line is often a function of therapist countertransference.

With defensive, help-rejecting, high-risk clients, acting on countertransference is almost inevitable. The trick is to recognize it when it happens. Let us look now at some of the patterns we tend to fall into and the complications that arise as a result.

## Trying Too Hard in the Therapy

The tendency to try too hard is a bit of an occupational hazard for people in the helping professions. As mentioned, most of us are in this field, at least in part, because of a strong interest in alleviating the suffering of others. The motivations underlying this interest can be complex and personal, and it is important that each clinician come to some understanding of what her own motivations are so that when an enactment occurs, it can be placed within the context of the therapist's personal, lived history.

We have all had the experience of finding ourselves in a therapy in which we are doing more than we should, we are too eager, making multiple attempts to engage the individual, yet working a good deal harder than the client. The problem with this state of affairs is that it ends up undermining the therapy process. It takes over, takes pressure off the individual, making it far too easy for patterns of avoidance to continue unchecked, ultimately serving to disempower (Herman, 1992) the client.

### *Nonverbal and Verbal Signals*

*Nonverbal* behaviors and internal emotional states can often be used as signals to the therapist that she is trying too hard. Over the course of one or many sessions, the clinician may notice herself responding to the client by sitting forward in her chair; using more gestures than usual; feeling tense, anxious or irritable; becoming frustrated with the client for, say, not trying harder. The therapist may find herself extending the session well beyond the end in a last-ditch effort to move things along, feeling a sense of mental exhaustion after the session has ended, or perhaps a sense of relief that it has ended.

A short while ago, a client who I had been working with for several months fell silent in midsentence during one particularly difficult session. Although she was pregnant and quickly approaching her due date, there were a number of important issues she still had not addressed, some of which were relevant to personal safety. During the sessions leading up to this point, she had been reluctant to discuss or even think about her child, neither her hopes and expectations nor her plans for mundane, but serious, matters such as daycare. When she stopped talking in midsentence during a difficult session, her voice trailing off as she looked away absently, I inquired regarding what happened just there. What was going on for her? After a moment's silence, she gazed up at me and pointed out that my foot was shaking again. I must have appeared bewildered, and in fact, I did wonder what she meant by "again," feeling a bit exposed, as if "caught in the act." Picking up on my confusion, she went on to explain herself: "You do that whenever you're about to lecture me."

The fact is, she was right. I *was* about to lecture her, and my foot *was* shaking. I have since recognized that I do this a lot. The point is that when we are made anxious by our clients, we convey this in our physical and behavioral responses to them. In this case, I was feeling the anxiety that my client could not bear to feel herself: anxiety about her becoming a mother. I would become quite troubled when I would consider her early history of abuse along with her many limitations, all in the context of her upcoming delivery. And, I would let myself get pulled into lecturing as a way of acting on my feelings. In so doing, I was undermining the process of therapy, taking care of her feelings *for her*. As long as I was there to feel anxious for her, she was off the hook.

Individuals in this clinical population, who turn away from difficult, painful feelings, can have this effect on the therapist; the clinician may experience the emotions the client cannot tolerate feeling himself. When we have the presence of mind to notice such processes in action, we can use our feelings and nonverbal behaviors as feedback, as signals to ourselves that something is amiss in the therapy.

*Verbal* communications in the therapist's language, speech mannerisms, and accompanying emotional states can also be used as signals to the therapist that she is engaged in a process of trying too hard. Sometimes, we find ourselves making attempts to fill silences by asking sequences of questions, relieving our own anxieties by making more suggestions than we normally do, lecturing or trying to educate, or becoming prescriptive in a way that feels excessive or unusual. We may rationalize our own behaviors to ourselves during the session, but later, feel exhausted from pushing so hard and find ourselves irritated with the client. Or, we may experience a sense of confusion about our reactions in the session, feeling like we were compelled to pursue a line of thinking for reasons unclear in the moment.

As described, when our interventions come from a place of acting on our own emotions or acting on the emotions our clients cannot tolerate experiencing for themselves, such countertransference reactions take away from the therapy, making it easy for the client to let responsibility for change lie in the therapist's hands, ultimately undermining client motivation and self-determination in the treatment. In describing the avoidant attachment pattern among adult survivors of incest, Alexander and Anderson (1994) emphasized the importance of allowing the client's anxieties to remain with the client instead of being inadvertently adopted by the therapist.

> Only by actually feeling the painful emotions in a supportive nurturing environment, can the client begin to reclaim her sorrow and anger arising from her parent's rejection of her. (p. 671)

### *When Trying Too Hard Means Trying to Repair*

Trying too hard can mean trying to "repair." In trying so hard that the therapist has taken responsibility to repair or fix a client (i.e., one who is presumed to be badly "damaged"), the clinician has begun to engage in patterns that ultimately undermine self-determination and do not serve the therapy well. The therapist has embarked on a process of client disempowerment (Herman, 1992).

Individuals in this clinical population tend to trigger emotional responses that draw the therapist into making attempts to repair, to fix the problem, the symptom, the wound, and so on. There can be a felt pressure on the clinician to act, to try excessively to make things better. When such a sentiment is strong, the therapist can easily cross into the realm of *acting on* her feelings, making attempts to manage personal, difficult emotions arising from the therapy by taking care of and by taking over. But in the process, the clinician may be undermining the treatment.

#### *Becoming Overly Invested in Outcomes*

One of the most important—yet often undervalued—tools that therapists have at their disposal is that of patience. Letting therapeutic processes unfold naturally means, as Axline (1969) asserted many years ago, therapy cannot be rushed. Building trust and reaching a point at which the clinician can function as a secure base (Bowlby, 1988), from which painful life experiences can be explored, depends on the therapist's skill at building a meaningful connection with the client. The building of that connection can take time. One way in which therapists make attempts to repair or fix their clients is by becoming *overly invested in outcome*, thereby undermining the therapy process.

In part, the tendency to become overly invested is fueled by the unfortunate reality of current mental health practice, that is, the pressure to move things along. Perhaps the client only has minimal coverage for outpatient treatment services, or perhaps the individual is being seen in a setting in which only brief approaches to psychotherapy are used, restricting the clinician's ability to build the treatment relationship as freely as she would otherwise. Such realities often place clear external pressures on the therapist to produce, to facilitate concrete symptomatic change, and to do so quickly.

However, much of the time, pressures on the clinician to invest so heavily in outcome are imposed from within the therapeutic interaction itself, imposed by dynamics that come about when working with this clinical population. With individuals who tend to be interpersonally distant and critical of others around them, there comes a more judgmental stance. There is often less tolerance within the therapeutic relationship for the process to unfold naturally, greater rigidity in client expectations, and less elasticity in relationships with others. Also, with the avoidance of attachment there can come a tendency to devalue the process of relationship building altogether.

The clinician may experience a kind of anxiety about whether she is doing enough, whether the therapy is effective enough, at times feeling a sense of pressure at having to prove herself and the worth of the treatment and at times getting drawn into feeling like she is letting the client down by not "fixing" the problem already.

It is easy then for the therapist to act in a desperate sort of way, becoming too invested in outcomes such as symptom change or problem resolution, giving serial "prescriptions," recommendations thought to help the presenting problem, suggestions that are often easily dismissed by the avoidant client for one reason or another. Or, the clinician may engage in a process of making serial interpretations, trying to give the individual explanations or answers, which, accurate and thoughtful as they may be, are often met by the client's perfunctory agreement at best.

In each of these circumstances, the therapist may be acting out of a kind of desperation, becoming overly invested in outcome, rather than taking a step back, letting the process unfold, reflecting on the interpersonal dynamics as they progress, putting attachment-related dynamics under the spotlight, and letting the client struggle with them.

### *Coming Into Conflict With Client Defensiveness*

Another way the therapist falls into attempts to repair the individual is by *reacting* a bit too strongly to *client defensiveness.* The clinician can get pulled into subtle disagreements, acting on built-up frustration in the interaction, letting the relationship take on a conflictual tone.

Client defensiveness can be hard to take. It can have a significant impact on the therapy and the therapist. With individuals who are reluctant to acknowledge moments of weakness, interpersonal vulnerability, and emotional pain, it is easy for the clinician to get drawn into a process of pushing a bit too hard, trying to convince the person of one viewpoint or another (e.g., "but that *must have* been so difficult on you"), reacting too strongly to defensiveness. In Chapter 3, we looked at the "I'm-no-victim" identity and the avoidant client's tendency to stay as far from the victim category as possible. We noted how it can be tempting to get pulled into an interaction in which the therapist, responding to elements of obvious victimization in the individual's history, comes into conflict with the person by perhaps invoking the "abuse," "trauma," or "survivor" label.

For the therapist, sitting in the midst of a defensive interaction can be difficult after a while. Here, the temptation may be to resolve feelings of discomfort on the clinician's part, sometimes by aggressively pushing onto the individual a viewpoint, an interpretation, psychoeducational advice, or presumed feelings. In such a context, client agreements, when they occur, are often hollow, such that the person may simply say the things the therapist "wants to hear" and then stop showing up for therapy altogether. Or equally problematic, client and therapist may find themselves in a kind of "mini-argument," leading the individual to feel irritated or misunderstood, to question the clinician's abilities and the enterprise of therapy altogether.

Many years ago, I had a session with a retired high school teacher who had contacted me for help in dealing with her sister. Well dressed and articulate, she had a list of questions that she had prepared. Reading them to me in succession off her clipboard, ticking them off as she went, it quickly felt more like a job interview than an initial session of psychotherapy. She inquired about my approach to treatment and whether I believed that people should "rehash" the past. She listed a series of topics that were off limits, including her separation from her husband and her history of childhood abuse, noting that these were topics she had "talked about already."

In the moment, my response was to get drawn in, to respond to her questions like a professor, as though all she needed was a little convincing about the benefits of therapy, but in the process I missed the more important emotional message that lay underneath her questions. That is, she was deeply afraid of engaging in the treatment process. Her turning of the tables early in the session was merely an initial show of strength. She needed this to feel in control, to cope with her uncomfortable feelings about starting therapy, to manage her feelings of anxiety about whether therapy was right for her and whether it would work for her, as well as her feelings of deep inadequacy about having become symptomatic in the first place. As described in Chapter 3, when individuals in this population become symptomatic, there is often a sense of inadequacy or personal failure, a sense of feeling disillusioned and disappointed with oneself.

Rather than connecting with her around the uncomfortable experience inherent in seeking help, I *reacted* to her initial show of strength and control, becoming defensive, trying to convince and push her into my way of seeing things as a means of coping with my own feelings in the moment and, along the way, coming to feel as inadequate as she did.

In this way, difficult emotional responses triggered in the clinician can sometimes be acted on in ways that derail the process. As mentioned, it is important that the therapist recognize such feelings as signals, as communications that something in the therapist has been powerfully affected by the client. They are opportunities to take a step back and reflect on the unfolding process. In this case, my own feelings of inadequacy could have served as windows into the emotional experience of the client and could have been instrumental in understanding what defensive effects her vulnerable feelings tend to have on her as well as what interpersonal effects her feelings provoke in her relationships with important others.

### *Becoming Overly Invested in Trauma-Related Material*

Another way the therapist can act on the urge to repair the client is by *rushing into trauma-related history* when the opportunity arises, by becoming overly invested in such material as a presumed way of making things better. Trauma-related experiences, and the process of revealing them, can seem so compelling that the therapist may get drawn in to the point of rushing their revelation in the therapy, acting on personal feelings that have been triggered along the way.

The revelation of traumatic experiences tends to yield strong emotional responses in the therapist. These can include a range of feelings, such as revulsion, disgust, and anger at the perpetrator. Equally important, however, are sentiments such as voyeuristic excitement, sexual arousal, and fascination (Herman, 1992). The clinician may feel, on one hand, repelled by such material, yet on the other "drawn toward" it.

To the extent that traumatic stories give rise to feelings of excitement or fascination, this is almost always experienced with ambivalence. Therapists may feel anxious and guilty for having such voyeuristic responses, as though they are doing something wrong, becoming tainted, or somehow aligning themselves with the perpetrator. Similarly, the clinician may have feelings of anger at the client for putting her in the position of having to endure or listen to such material in the first place, feeling victimized in some way.

Still, the sense of having gotten to "something important" when trauma-related material arises can be compelling for the therapist, sometimes making it difficult to hold back a feeling of internal excitement. This sentiment as well comes with ambivalence as the clinician may feel a bit "like a vulture," eager to capitalize on the opportunity, eager to fully unpack the meaning of traumatic events that, perhaps, had not come up before or that the client had previously felt too guarded to discuss.

In addition to feelings of fascination with traumatic material per se, the process by which these stories come up has an important effect on the therapist. Revealing and talking about traumatic experiences can take on a special meaning within the therapeutic relationship, leading to a sense of connection with the client. Such a connection can be gratifying for the therapist. Dalenberg (2000) wrote:

> As therapist and client discuss great adversity, the painful events can become a shared burden. The members of the dyad often become bonded through their (possibly secret or illicit) knowledge of the trauma and at times through their joint identification with the trauma.

> . . . The telling of the story intensifies this connection in cases in which the members of the dyad have a good empathic connection. (p. 202)

Such a therapeutic connection has a particularly high premium when working with individuals in this clinical population, for whom early in the process closeness can seem unlikely ever to take shape. When the avoidant client starts to address trauma-related experiences, the therapist can feel relief, excitement, satisfaction, and even a sense of self-importance in the way that one does in knowing that they have been entrusted with some important information. Thus, this special connection with the client can feel gratifying. And, it is easy for the clinician to become drawn in by the joint process of telling and hearing about trauma-related experiences, to be affected and personally moved by a newly found connection with the client.

The therapist's overinvestment in trauma-related material can become problematic for the treatment when it means uncovering or opening up too quickly. Moving into trauma revelations can be detrimental if it occurs before the client is ready or before the relationship can tolerate it.

Those of us who self-identify as having a special interest in the psychotherapy of trauma survivors may consider ourselves comfortable working with trauma-related experiences and may feel motivated to address them in the treatment. Knowing very well that our clients' stories have often been ignored by, say, nonoffending caregivers, professionals, and other bystanders, we may find ourselves in the position of trying to undo or fix the hurt that our clients have experienced for so long, so there can be a strong inclination to help, reparent (Pearlman & Courtois, 2005), or rescue the individual from continued suffering by bringing trauma-related material into the open. However, this wish on the therapist's part may inadvertently undermine the therapy process when the foundation for a therapeutic alliance has not yet been built.

As discussed in previous chapters, the establishment of a reliable, collaborative relationship is critical to the therapy. There must be a sense of safety and security. Without the building of an alliance between therapist and client, without the sense that the treatment environment is emotionally safe, there can be no basis for trust. And although trust in the therapeutic relationship may be frightening in its own right—as it can raise feelings of vulnerability and dependency—without it, there is no legitimate basis on which to ask the client to take the emotional risks necessary to face traumatic experiences. When the therapist becomes focused or invested in traumatic material before building basic trust in the therapeutic relationship, she is really asking the client to move too quickly.

When I was in graduate school, I worked with a young woman who presented with a traumatic history that had a strong impact on me. When Ayana came to the training clinic for therapy, she had been in a depression for at least 8 months following her mother's funeral. Years earlier, she had cut off all contact with her family and was just starting to allow her mother back into her life. Her mother had made a number of previous attempts to get in touch with her, but Ayana had rebuffed all such efforts until she became pregnant with her first child. After discussing it with her husband, she made the decision to "just forget about" the terrible abuse she had experienced when she was younger, inviting her mother to her child's baptism.

The ceremony was by her accounts unremarkable, but afterward, when her mother made the drive across the state highway to return home, she lost control of the vehicle and was killed in a car accident. It was clear that Ayana did not know whom to blame for her mother's death, vacillating between at times blaming herself, at times her mother, and at times blaming her infant daughter. In her distress, she was experiencing enormous difficulty with the role of parenting, unable to form a proper attachment with her child.

I found her story touching, and I became focused on the details: her history of growing up in an unstable region of Africa; the loss of her entire family except for her mother to various forms of political terror, including disappearances and executions; her being sexually assaulted in her early 20s by her mother's then-boyfriend, and so on. During one of her assessment sessions, I took so many notes, detailing so many aspects of her traumatic history, that I actually developed a cramp in my hand from all the writing.

In total, I had only three sessions with her before she dropped out of treatment for reasons unclear at the time. Although my fascination with her story of traumatic loss was likely the main reason for our having rushed into trauma-related material as we had, it is also likely that a significant urge to reveal came from the client herself in a desperate attempt to purge herself of guilt and self-blame over the loss. In either case, what *was* lacking from the process was a sufficiently strong alliance and an adequately developed sense of trust and safety in the therapeutic environment prior to immersing us both in trauma-related material. In reflecting on the case afterward, it seemed that had I slowed the process; had I exercised more restraint and given her permission to do the same, the process of opening up would have been less overwhelming to her, and she might have been less inclined to drop out of treatment early.

It was only a couple of years later that I read the following passage in *Trauma and Recovery* (Herman, 1992):

> Though the single most common therapeutic error is avoidance of the traumatic material, probably the second most common error is premature or precipitate engagement in exploratory work, without sufficient attention to the tasks of establishing safety and securing a therapeutic alliance. Patients at times insist upon plunging into graphic, detailed descriptions of their traumatic experiences, in the belief that simply pouring out the story will solve all their problems. At the root of this belief is the fantasy of a violent cathartic cure which will get rid of the trauma once and for all. (p. 172)

### *When Trying Too Hard Means Trying to Accommodate*

At times we are drawn in by a very different pattern. Rather than trying to repair the client and his many wounds, we are pulled into a position of trying to *accommodate* the individual.

In response to client expressions of need, we may find ourselves pulled into a position of acquiescence: giving in, colluding. The therapist may feel compelled to give in to demands, to indulge the person's explicit or implicit requests for special regard, time, and attention, even at the risk of crossing usual therapeutic boundaries. The clinician may also get drawn into a pattern of colluding with the client's defenses, not wanting to upset the status quo, evading such difficult issues as traumatic emotional experiences, attachment-related distress, or self-defeating coping patterns. As therapists, this pattern of trying to accommodate is one to which we may be susceptible, particularly when we feel intimidated or "lesser than" in the interaction.

#### *Feeling Intimidated: Giving in to Demands*

When client self-portrayal emphasizes especially those elements of avoidant attachment that convey the appearance of strength and invulnerability, it is easy for the clinician to miss the hurt that lies below and to respond instead to the portrayed image, to the "false self" (Masterson, 1985; Winnicott, 1960/1965), becoming unduly drawn in by the individual's image of self as strong. The therapist may feel a *sense of intimidation* (Mills, 2005) in the client's presence, and an imbalance can quickly develop in the therapeutic relationship. Feelings of inadequacy, a sense of being lesser than the individual may be provoked, and the therapist can get drawn into a pattern of giving in to demands, perhaps explicitly by relaxing therapeutic boundaries, or perhaps implicitly by becoming intrigued by idealized stories or images, giving in to the client's wish for the clinician's special attention.

The therapist may even become interested and intrigued by the compensatory strengths and competencies the client has come to use in his life. In this case, she may be susceptible to putting the individual up on a pedestal, to viewing the person as special in some way, "a real survivor," "a portrait of strength." This is particularly true when something in the client's presentation touches a personal chord in the clinician, yielding in her feelings of admiration and envy. The therapist may come to overlook key aspects of client vulnerability and dependency.

In attempting to emphasize strength and competence, individuals who are avoidant of attachment often demonstrate themes in their content that place weight on personal achievement (George & West, 2001), along with material examples of success, such as wealth, degrees, and professional designations. Such content can trigger a variety of different responses, depending on the clinician's history and personal vulnerabilities. However, in response to stereotypic demonstrations of competence, success, and strength, it is not unusual that feelings of envy and admiration be stirred, so that the therapist, in the interaction, may become caught up in her own feelings of intimidation and inadequacy, incapable of seeing client vulnerabilities just below the surface.

The client's emphasis on strength may also portray an image of resilience, one suggesting that the individual has already overcome the effects of his traumatic past, or that he is impressive and special, having survived as he has. The resilient pattern has been described in a number of cases (Higgins, 1994b; Luthar, Cicchetti, & Becker, 2000), including those of individuals with histories of trauma who nevertheless demonstrate security of attachment in adulthood, the so-called earned secure (Pearson, Cohn, Cowan, & Cowan, 1994; Roisman, Padron, Sroufe, & Egeland, 2002). It is not unusual to see those who have overcome adversity with a sense of admiration, to view them as "brave" and as "having a positive attitude." However, as discussed in Chapters 2 and 4, clients who are avoidant of attachment are not, in fact, resilient, as they are highly susceptible to defensive breakdown and to the expression of psychiatric symptomatology in the face of situational stress and attachment-related distress. Yet, when colored by interesting content—stories of personal misfortune along-side acts of bravery, philanthropy, optimism, and self-sacrifice—it is easy to get drawn into a position of viewing the client with admiration.

When the therapist reacts to client assertions of strength by experiencing feelings of intimidation or inadequacy in his presence, she has been drawn into a pattern of interaction that may be all too common in the individual's daily life. The clinician is experiencing feelings that are defensively designed to keep the client safely above others. Such a process reifies an illusory sense of power and control. Further, it precludes the development of true intimacy, with the insidious effects of therapist and client being caught up in a collusion that fails to address and integrate trauma-related feelings of hurt and vulnerability.

Acting on feelings of intimidation can lead to a pattern of giving in under the weight of client demands, of having a "special set of rules" for this client, of trying to accommodate the individual. The therapist may compromise in ways that are uncharacteristic or excessive relative to her normal practice: unduly giving in to the client on issues such as late cancellations, no shows, fee reductions, late sessions, weekend appointments, and running over time. The clinician may find herself continuing with compromising patterns of behavior despite feeling resentful, while rationalizing to herself that the therapeutic relationship is too fragile to withstand further limit setting. She may feel anxious at the prospect of standing up to the client's demands when colleagues or supervisors advise her to, yet feel uneasy about the compromises she has already made.

What makes this pattern especially problematic is that it represents a buckling of the therapeutic frame. It conveys inconsistency, a certain weakness in the therapeutic environment as secure, as one that is strong and safe enough to provide containment. To make the therapeutic environment a secure base, the clinician must be "strong enough" to tolerate affects that, up to now, have been intolerable to the client and to others.

For the therapist, this means guarding the therapeutic frame. It means staying consistent, keeping good boundaries, feeling licensed to decline client requests that "cross the line," noticing moments of feeling lesser than or inadequate in the individual's presence, and thinking about how such feelings play out in the client's relationships with others, but resisting the temptation to give in to demands out of feelings of intimidation.

### *Colluding With Avoidant Defenses*

As mentioned, there are times that we are drawn into a pattern of disproportionate accommodation. In response to explicit or implicit expressions of need, we may find ourselves in a position of acquiescence, that is, giving in to client demands, and accommodating in ways that may not be characteristic of our more usual approach in psychotherapy. In this regard, we may fall into a pattern of colluding with client defenses, going along with avoidant coping patterns, even when we recognize that it may not be what the individual really needs. In the present context, *collusion* amounts to a tacit agreement between therapist and client to evade discussion of traumatic experiences and attachment-related distress, domains that are emotionally painful and that provoke a sense of personal vulnerability.

The tendency toward therapist avoidance regarding the revelation of trauma-related material has been described widely. For example, Wilson, Lindy, and Raphael (1994) noted that the clinician may easily get drawn into an interaction in which traumatic material is avoided because doing so preserves a world-view that life is decent and just.

> The client's traumatic stressors often include loss, disillusionment, and threat to life. Hearing about these experiences commonly evokes unpleasant affects, such as horror, dread, fear, hostility, or vengeance. Therapists unconsciously, and in order to avoid pain and preserve their world view, distance themselves from this affect. ( p. 41)

Thus, the therapist is motivated by internal pressures to avoid material that feels personally threatening. Even more insidious, however, is the pattern of "mutual avoidance" (Alexander & Anderson, 1994), discussed in Chapters 2 and 3, the tacit agreement that occurs in the space *between* therapist and client. Through repeated interaction in which personal inquiries by the therapist are met with a sense of discomfort, minimization, and emotional detachment, therapist and client come to co-construct a climate of progressive accommodation to client avoidant defenses.

Of course, this collusion goes both ways. While therapists accommodate to client avoidance, clients accommodate to therapist avoidance as well. In her study on countertransference and the treatment of trauma, Dalenberg (2000) found that many individuals went through a process of actually protecting their therapists from trauma revelations as a number of the clinicians avoided, misheard, and minimized such material. Similarly, Cloitre et al. noted the tendency for some clinicians to subtly redirect individuals away from such experiences, and that clients "may take redirection from a therapist as a message that the therapist can't manage hearing about their abuse" (2006, p. 98). Disentangling the source of avoidance can quickly become a chicken–egg matter. The reality is that the therapist–client dyad is a dynamic relationship, like any other, in which tacit rules of exchange come to be generated progressively, through actual interactions.

In working with individuals in this clinical population, it is not uncommon that psychotherapy dyads find themselves in tacit agreement not to cross into certain difficult areas. These may include such content domains as trauma-related stories brought up in earlier sessions; material that could be construed as trauma-related but has not been openly acknowledged as such; current or past losses that are as yet unmourned and unresolved; and stresses on the therapeutic relationship that occur as a consequence of closeness and distancing maneuvers. This last pattern is one of the most difficult content areas to cross into as it means directly looking at the therapy relationship. It means, for example, looking at what it is about the client that makes trust and vulnerability so uncomfortable and what it is about the therapist that provokes relational anxieties and fears.

For the clinician, the ability to catch herself engaging in mutual avoidance is a difficult, but important, aspect of treatment. To this end, it is helpful when the therapist makes active attempts to *notice and understand* her own feelings, particularly those contributing to avoidance. She can challenge herself to look at the role her anxieties may play. As detailed in Chapter 3, such sentiments include fear of "intruding" on the privacy of others, guilt for asking upsetting or painful questions, and discomfort with all things repulsive, disgusting, and disturbing. Anxieties in any of these areas can make it difficult for the clinician to bear witness to her client's painful story. One of the challenges I find in working with supervisees is in helping them face the uncomfortable feelings that arise for them as traumatic material arises for their clients. As noted, in the present context, collusion amounts to a tacit agreement between therapist and client to evade discussion of traumatic experiences and attachment-related distress. As therapists, understanding such collusion means understanding our personal anxieties about pursuing traumatic material when it arises in the treatment.

## Giving Up on the Therapy

To this point, we have been discussing responses that are typical of the clinician who gets unduly *drawn in*, the therapist who becomes activated by the client in one way or another. As uncomfortable feelings surface in response to certain aspects of the person's presentation, the clinician may react in ways that pull her in, with such reactions being attempts to manage the difficult feelings that have been triggered. However, individuals in this clinical population can also provoke responses of a very different nature. When the clinician comes to feel devalued or unimportant, when she perceives the therapy as dispensable or irrelevant to the client, this may pull for a response in the other direction. Instead of becoming overly invested in the treatment process, instead of getting drawn in, the clinician may feel repelled and may *draw away*. In so doing, she pulls back from the individual and begins to give up on the therapeutic relationship.

Feelings of frustration with the treatment of a reluctant client may lead to this kind of backing away. It may appear in the therapist in the form of passive resignation, fatigue, or withdrawal (Lindy & Wilson, 1994; Wilson et al., 1994), or it may be marked by more active feelings such as resentment, anger, disgust, and dislike, peppered by internal commentary about the therapy being "a waste of time" and the like. In either case, the therapist has either implicitly or explicitly given up on the client and on the treatment, deciding, on some level, no longer to engage in the process, having lost hope regarding the individual's prospect for change through psychotherapy.

When such a process takes place, therapist feelings have become activated by something in the client's presentation or by the clinician's own personal experiences, vulnerabilities, and attachment patterns, leading to a progressive or sudden disengagement from the therapy.

## *When We Become Disengaged*

When the clinician does not experience the therapy as being *used* by the client in any meaningful sense, it is easy for her to become discouraged. Therapist disengagement suggests a kind of retreat, a pulling back, sometimes in resignation. Along with a sense of not feeling useful to the client, there is a tendency to see the therapy as somehow lacking. The clinician may perceive a lack of progress, direction, or purpose and may consider the therapy to be altogether lacking in substance. A perception that the treatment is not being used in any meaningful sense can have an enormous impact on the therapist's connection to the process.

We have all encountered a therapy that does not appear to move forward, one in which we see the client engaging in repetitive patterns of self-defeating behavior, recounting similar themes or content in a perpetual manner. Perhaps we cannot find a purpose or direction in the treatment; the sessions may have a tendency to meander along aimlessly as if groping about for something of substance. Or, perhaps we find ourselves drumming up the same reflections, observations, or interpretations that we have made before with the client, with the interaction lacking a sense of immediacy or freshness.

### *Verbal and Nonverbal Signs of Disengagement*

A number of verbal and nonverbal behaviors characterize the therapist disengagement that can arise in such circumstances. During sessions, the clinician may find her attention wandering; she may find herself distracted by personal matters, becoming uninterested or bored, furtively watching the clock. She may feel excessively fidgety, shifting about more than usual, sometimes in an effort to keep her eyes open. On those occasions that the client is late, the therapist may catch herself secretly wishing the individual would not show up at all, almost feeling disappointed when, at last, he arrives, or the clinician may find that she is starting sessions late, ending early, or finding other ways to "shave off" some of the time.

Other therapist behaviors indicative of disengagement are seen when the clinician stops guarding the therapeutic frame, allowing boundaries to be broken by using session time to chit-chat with the client in a way that goes beyond usual rapport building, becoming interested in material irrelevant to the treatment, or the therapist may stop protecting the time by, say, taking calls during the session. She may begin to imagine that surely a different clinician would work better with this person, perhaps wondering about possible colleagues to hand the client off to. Or, she may all too easily let the individual off the hook, failing to call him out on his behavior once a pattern of cancelling, lateness, and not showing up has begun.

Instead of noticing and addressing distancing patterns, she may respond by writing the client off or by forgetting about him, letting the therapy just "fizzle away," without any clear sense of how that happened, how it is that the client is not coming in anymore.

### *The Effect of Intellectualization on the Therapist*

An important contributor to therapist disengagement is client defensiveness. For many clinicians, excessive intellectualization can be hard to endure. The individual who is avoidant of attachment tends to be detached from his emotional experiences, particularly those provoking traumatic distress, attachment-related threat, or feelings of rejection, sadness, and neediness. When the client engages excessively in intellectualization, he brings into the therapy the implied message that emotions are uncomfortable.

We often see a tendency toward therapist disengagement when working with clients who rely heavily on intellectualized speech or activity, with the individual focusing attention on the cognitive rather than on the emotional elements of experience. Recall that Bowlby (1980) thought of this as a form of diversion, noting that sometimes intellectual pursuits may become so consuming that they monopolize the person's energy, systematically excluding attachment-related experience from processing, for example, changing topics toward non-threatening issues, excessive focus on work at the expense of relationships, or tremendous time spent on activity-centered friendships.

With individuals who rely heavily on intellectualization, the challenge for the therapist is to refrain from *closing off.* It is easy for the clinician to become uninterested or distant, "somewhere else" during the session (Mohr et al., 2005), particularly if the therapist's natural inclination is to engage with others more on affective or relational terms. By closing off, the clinician is accommodating to the individual's tendency to turn away from attachment-related experiences and emotions, letting the client remain in an avoidant "loop," with the therapist managing personal feelings by emotionally disengaging from the process altogether.

### *The Effect of Talking Around on the Therapist*

As stated, client defensiveness is an important contributor to therapist disengagement. Like intellectualization, it can also be difficult to contend with excessive talking around (see Chapter 1). By discussing and focusing attention on non-attachment-related issues, often at considerable length, the client evades the more emotionally painful attachment-related experiences. The individual may very well appear active in the session, presenting various concerns and difficulties, discussing matters that are consequential and that feel pressing, while still diverting attention away from attachment-related hurts and conflicts. In this way, talking around may be used as a means of avoiding issues that are much more difficult to address.

A danger for the clinician is in becoming *complacent.* With such avoidant clients as those who have the ability to "fill the silence," sessions sometimes have a way of turning into repetitive descriptions of interpersonal events, laden with minutiae. In comparison to the individual who struggles with knowing what to discuss in session, the avoidant client who uses talking around may represent somewhat of a relief to the clinician, at least initially, as the individual requires less effort on the therapist's part simply to keep the session moving along. Nevertheless, as sessions continue to appear as two-dimensional soliloquies in which the client talks around attachment-related issues, the clinician may settle into a certain disengaged complacence, letting this state of affairs continue indefinitely, all the while moving further away from the therapeutic process.

Sometimes talking around can appear in more subtle ways, and effects on the therapist can be more subtle as well. When the client is creative, humorous, or otherwise interesting, this can yield a process of disengagement that is much harder to spot. That is, through interesting discussion, bright, creative clients can insidiously lead the therapist away from the task at hand, distracting from the treatment by engaging on culturally or generationally congruent interests. Verbally exhibitionistic clients can do likewise by using sexually-related or drug-related language and by recounting interesting personal anecdotes, which have the effect of "entertaining" or arousing the curiosities of the therapist.

In each of these cases, as narratives appear with more emotionally toned content and as content becomes more inherently interesting, it may be less apparent that the client is, in fact, talking around attachment-related issues. And as the therapist breaks the therapeutic frame by becoming intrigued by such material, she has unwittingly disengaged from her proper role.

The challenge for the clinician is in not letting the therapeutic interaction transform into social interaction or voyeuristic gratification, not letting surface talkativeness, sociability, chit-chatty expressiveness, and interesting anecdotes divert attention from the therapeutic task. Otherwise, in time, such interaction can lead to therapist disengagement from her role and from the treatment.

### *Therapist Disengagement and Trauma*

It is important to consider the broader implication of therapist disengagement for individuals in this clinical population. Insofar as disengagement represents a type of backing away from the therapeutic relationship, it can replicate the inaction or indifference often seen in bystander responses to cases of trauma.

Over the course of treatment, therapeutic interactions often have a tendency to mirror a number of simultaneous conflicts connected to traumatic experiences, and the clinician and client can take on any number of roles in the transference, such as persecutor, rescuer, victim (Liotti, 2004). To the extent that the therapist, in part, can also take on the role of *witness* and to the extent that psychotherapy, in part, serves to bear witness to experiences that seem unbelievable or intolerable, when the clinician disengages from the treatment, this can constitute a type of betrayal. That is, the therapist, the one whose role is to bear witness to client suffering, has essentially abandoned her therapeutic function.

In retreating from the treatment process and from the therapeutic relationship, the clinician is letting down the individual in the same way the nonoffending parent does when failing to stand by the child, when failing to protect. And, even though the client's natural inclination is toward minimizing trauma-related experience (along with minimizing the importance of therapy and the therapist), when the clinician reacts accordingly, when she takes on a position of disengagement and effectively follows suit, she unwittingly abandons the therapy and betrays the client.

## *When We Dislike or Hate the Client*

As described, the therapist may, at times, draw back from the client and from the therapeutic relationship. In considering the process of giving up on the therapy, we have so far discussed the pattern of therapist disengagement, how the clinician may close off her feelings or become complacent, how she may retreat from the therapeutic process. But sometimes, giving up can come from quite a different place, one of overwhelmingly strong therapist feelings. Through the course of treatment, the clinician may come to experience such sentiments toward the individual as anger, disgust, dislike, and hate, and rather than letting the therapy whither away, there is a more direct wish to somehow make it end. When this occurs, therapist feelings have become affected, usually by something in the client's presentation or by the clinician's personal experiences, vulnerabilities, and attachment patterns. The risk is that such feelings may prompt therapist responses that serve to undermine the therapeutic process.

Some people are terribly difficult to like, no matter how hard we may try. Disliking our clients is not so easy to admit. Certainly, for some clinicians, there may be relatively little discomfort in knowing that a particular individual has provoked, say, feelings of anger. For others, even an admission such as this may raise anxieties about being too harsh or aggressive. And for many, there are feelings our clients trigger in us that we would really rather not think about at all, feelings such as disgust, contempt, and hatred.

Given the complex mix of feelings provoked in us by the traumatic experiences of our clients, the reality is that we do not always identify with the victim. At times, we instead experience various *identifications with the perpetrator*. For example, we may find ourselves blaming or judging the victim (Courtois, 1988; Dalenberg, 2000), perhaps becoming unconcerned or reacting internally in a manner that seems much harder or less caring than usual.

As therapists who work with adults who have been victimized, such sentiments may be hard to admit. Most of us feel much more comfortable in the role of nurturer, and strong negative feelings toward our clients do not fit in so easily. Nevertheless, if we do not accept the reality of our uncomfortable, "uglier" feelings, if we do not work to understand their meaning and significance, we run the risk of acting on them and in the end damaging the treatment process.

Acting on such feelings as they surface is one way we come to write off the client and ultimately give up on the therapy. In a classic paper on countertransference, Winnicott described how some clients can raise our most powerful, "primitive" feelings. He noted that on one hand, we are under intense strain to keep such feelings under control, but on the other, we can only do so by becoming aware of them. Thus, the therapist "is best forewarned and forearmed" (1947/1975, p. 196).

With some clients, it may be tempting to act on the strong, negative emotions that get stirred in us, but in so doing, we might react dismissively, essentially writing the person off. This often occurs with individuals diagnosed with personality disorders. With such clients, the therapist may easily feel rejected, manipulated, smothered, mistreated, and may come to use labeling pejoratively: "She's *so* borderline," "He's nothing but a narcissist," and so on. Acting on strong, negative emotions is also not uncommon with perpetrators of sexual abuse, with whom it is normal for the therapist to experience uncomfortable feelings such as fear, anxiety, contempt, and revulsion.

With one client, a perpetrator who himself had been sexually abused as a child, my biggest challenge was in resisting the temptation to act on feelings of disgust. This was even more difficult given his avoidant, defensive stance. During sessions, I would find myself feeling repulsed even by minor features in his presentation, the smell of his aftershave or deodorant, the fact that his fingernails were bitten, and so on. Even the way he dressed became, in some sense, irritating to me.

It was only once I presented the case to a colleague that I came to understand just how strong my feelings toward him really were, how I had been subtly acting on my feelings of disgust. For example, normally I take a careful developmental history in the early stages of treatment. In the process of doing so, I often find that it increases not only my understanding but also my sense of connection with the individual. However, with this particular client, I had conspicuously sidestepped the process. My narrow knowledge of this individual's history even after a few months of treatment became clear when I presented the case to a colleague. She rightly suggested that it was perhaps my way of avoiding getting to know him all that well, and therefore avoiding an uncomfortable sense of connection with him. It was as though I feared that by association, I would become somehow tarnished or morally tainted. Essentially, I had all but written him off, secretly hoping he would drop out of treatment on his own.

On my colleague's advice, I challenged myself to try to empathize with his sense of loss, one of his qualities to which I could find some personal connection. After allegations were made against him, he had, in fact, lost everything: his wife of many years, custody and access to their children, his job. Still, as I made what amounted to half-hearted attempts to connect with this sense of loss, I could not stop thinking that he "got what he deserved" and found myself unable to get past my own anxieties. Soon after, the client dropped out of treatment on his own. In this way, acting on my feelings served to undermine the therapeutic process.

One final point I would like to make in regard to feelings of dislike or hate is that such feelings almost always come with a degree of ambivalence; therefore, they also give rise to defensive rebound effects. At different points in the relationship, as the therapist becomes uncomfortable with the strong negative emotions that have been triggered in her, she may make attempts to undo such feelings or make up for them. Wilson et al. (1994) and Tansey and Burke (1989) described such defensive processes in detail. Tansey and Burke wrote: "This defensive posture . . . may surface in the therapist's becoming 'too nice' in an attempt to compensate for unconscious guilt, anger, or sadistic impulses toward a patient" (p. 82).

For the therapist working with individuals who have experienced trauma, identification with the perpetrator brings a sense of uneasiness and usually comes with a certain measure of guilt and anxiety. Different attempts in the clinician to make up for these uncomfortable feelings may take place. And, ambivalent reactions can be seen in the therapist who, on one hand, may feel a number of negative emotions toward the client but, on the other hand, may feel compelled to "bend over backward" for the individual, for example, becoming excessively "nice," failing to challenge the client when necessary, and giving in to client demands in many of the ways described in this chapter. For this reason, it is important that the clinician keep aware of feelings like anger, disgust, and dislike as such feelings may lead to a variety of therapist responses that may have different appearances in different contexts.

## Summing Up

In discussing therapist countertransference, we began the chapter by wondering about clinician motivation for this kind of work. Those who do psychotherapy with traumatized adults may be motivated by a number of factors associated with the helping role. Yet, as discussed throughout, individuals in this clinical population struggle with the very idea of relying on the therapist.

Therapist reactions to help-rejecting, defensive behavior have a strong impact on the treatment. They may include feelings of rejection, hurt, a sense of incompetence, and self-doubt. The feelings that get provoked in the clinician are useful and can be used as a signal that something important has been triggered. The clinician must work to recognize such feelings when they occur and to use them in the service of the therapy. Difficulties arise not because of the feelings that get provoked in the therapist, but because she has acted on those feelings. With defensive, high-risk clients, acting on countertransference is almost inevitable. The important thing is to recognize it when it happens.

A common therapist pattern is to *try too hard*, which can have the unintended effects of taking over, undermining the treatment process and disempowering the client. Nonverbal and verbal behaviors, along with their accompanying internal emotional states, can be used as signals to the therapist that she is trying too hard.

When the clinician tries to *repair*, she has become drawn into attempts to fix the problem. There is felt pressure on the clinician to act, to somehow find a way to make things better. When such a sentiment is strong, the therapist can easily cross into acting on her feelings, making attempts to manage her own emotions arising from the therapy by taking over, but in the process, the clinician may be undermining the treatment. The therapist may make attempts to repair or fix the client by becoming *overly invested in outcome*. She may experience a kind of anxiety about whether she is doing enough, feeling a sense of pressure at having to prove herself and the worth of the treatment. She may also fall into attempts to repair the client by *reacting* a bit too strongly to *client defensiveness*, getting pulled into subtle disagreements, aggressively pushing onto the client a viewpoint, presumed feelings, and so on. In addition, the clinician may act on the urge to repair the client by *rushing into trauma-related material,* eager to unpack trauma-related revelations as they arise, experiencing gratification from the closer connection that comes with such discussion in therapy. Moving into trauma-related material can be detrimental if it occurs before the client is ready or before the therapeutic relationship can tolerate it.

When the clinician excessively *accommodates,* she finds herself pulled into a position of acquiescence, giving in to demands for special regard, time, attention, and so on, even at the risk of crossing usual therapeutic boundaries. Patterns of excessive accommodation sometimes come about due to feelings of *intimidation.* When the therapist experiences a sense of inadequacy, of being lesser than, or when feelings of envy or admiration are stirred, she may get drawn into such patterns. Patterns of excessive accommodation may also come about through a process of *collusion* with client defenses. As described in previous chapters, mutual avoidance amounts to a tacit agreement between therapist and client to evade discussion of traumatic experiences and attachment-related distress. For the clinician, understanding this pattern means understanding her own anxieties about pursuing traumatic material as it arises. Thus, it is helpful when the therapist makes active attempts to notice and understand these anxieties and the ways they contribute to avoidance in the treatment.

Turning to a very different kind of process, the therapist may come to *give up* on the treatment. Rather than becoming drawn in, the clinician may feel repelled by the client, may lose hope regarding the individual's prospect for change, and may draw away. Therapist tendency to give up may be seen in a progressive *disengagement* from the therapy, often in response to not feeling used by the client. A number of verbal and nonverbal behaviors characterize therapist disengagement, including, for example, letting the individual off the hook once a pattern of lateness, failing to show up, and so on has begun. Therapist disengagement may be seen when working with clients who rely heavily on intellectualized speech or activity. With such individuals, the challenge for the therapist is to refrain from *closing off*, becoming uninterested or distant during the session. Therapist disengagement may also be seen with the client who talks around attachment-related issues, with the clinician settling into a disengaged *complacence*. It is important to consider the broader implication of therapist disengagement for clients with histories of trauma. Insofar as it represents a backing away from the therapeutic relationship, disengagement can replicate the inaction seen in bystander responses to traumatic events.

Finally, the clinician may give up on the therapy by coming to *dislike* or hate the client. When we identify with the perpetrator, we may find ourselves blaming or judging the victim or reacting in a way that seems less caring than usual. Such sentiments may be difficult to admit as most therapists feel more comfortable in the role of nurturer. Unless we notice and accept the reality of our "uglier" feelings, we run the risk of acting on them by, say, reacting dismissively or writing the client off. Feelings of dislike or hate almost always come with a degree of ambivalence and therefore give rise to defensive rebound effects by which the clinician may attempt to make up for her uncomfortable feelings by bending over backward or excessively giving in to client demands.

CHAPTER 7

# Looking at the Treatment Components Together: The Case of Madeline

One of the challenges faced by clinicians learning psychotherapy is that it is often hard to visualize how the treatment process will look in practice. This is certainly the case for the novice, but even when highly experienced therapists are exposed to a somewhat different way of working, it may be hard to imagine how exactly the components all fit together. On more than one occasion, I have had the experience of sitting at a conference on, say, a treatment program or a clinical population that was new to me, finding that once I saw the process unfold across a session or two of treatment, the suggested approach became much clearer. Sometimes, the challenge may be less about learning something entirely new, as trying to imagine how an approach could possibly work in the "real world." Theoretical clients (who say all the right things) respond very differently from real ones, who often go off track, forget insights they made just a week earlier, and sometimes decide to drop out just as they begin making some progress.

This chapter, in which the focus is on one case in detail, provides the opportunity to review several of the interventions discussed previously. I ask the reader to notice a few things in particular: examples of client emotional expressiveness, moments marked by client vulnerability in relation to the clinician, points of connection or disconnection between client and therapist, and places where you (if you had been the clinician) would *feel* something strongly (e.g., annoyance, excitement, boredom, and so on).

---

Madeline was a 26-year-old French-Canadian-born business student who came to treatment 6 months after her partner, Kevin, ended their 3-year relationship. After the breakup, Madeline temporarily moved back in with her parents and her 19-year-old sister. Having moved back for financial reasons, she soon found it unbearable to live at home. When symptoms of clinical depression began to worsen, she was referred to me for psychotherapy. Through much of our work, she was also on a selective serotonin reuptake inhibitor (SSRI) antidepressant. Although she found the medication helpful, she felt quite humiliated and ashamed for not having, in her words, "the willpower" to fix her own problems without needing psychiatric medication to help her do so.

Madeline's pattern of avoidant attachment included the tendency to idealize her father, the use of minimization as a defense, a pattern of downplaying painful early experiences, and a propensity to view herself as independent, strong, and normal. She also demonstrated the tendency to sidestep attachment-related hurts by using humor to keep things light. Notably, she was somewhat critical of her mother, considering her to have been "weak and frightened" much of the time. However, she justified this behavior as being consistent with how women have always been taught to behave in society at large.

During the first few sessions of psychotherapy, she reported a history of sexual abuse from her father, although she did not refer to it in such terms. He would make numerous advances toward her, including touching her breasts, groping her, asking to photograph her in the nude, and so on, all starting during her preteen years. These often occurred when mother was not around, sometimes when he was under the influence of alcohol and marijuana, and continued on and off into Madeline's midadolescence. Of note, she was also sexually assaulted in a number of relationships as a teenager and as a young adult, by both men and women, and was once assaulted by an unlicensed health care professional. Importantly, she apparently had been brought in for psychotherapy as a teenager, but the ongoing sexual abuse from her father was never reported to authorities for reasons that were unclear.

By the second month of therapy, she made the decision to move out of her family home despite the cost, and found an apartment to share with two other women from her business program. Soon after, she decided to follow a friend's advice and confront her father with respect to his prior sexual behavior toward her.

The current session took place about 5 months into treatment. The transcript picks up about one third of the way into the session. This segment follows a discussion of her difficulties in school as a teenager, how she went through a rebellious period in high school when she would "party" (alcohol and marijuana) a lot, how she would get brought in to see the guidance counselor because of her academic difficulties, and how as an adolescent she often felt uncomfortable talking to adults, including the psychotherapist whom she saw for about a year during that difficult time of her life.

---

[one third of the way into the session]

***Madeline:*** There were lots of things I had trouble talking about. Sometimes, I would just sit there, and Dr. Dave would stare, like, look at me, and not say anything. Sometimes, he would ask things that provoked me into talking. But I had a really bad attitude, and I thought "go ahead and make me. I'm not playing along," like . . . I was a very annoying person to be around. I mean, basically because it was kinda fun to do. But I'm sure he found me *really* annoying. He wrote this counseling book or something. I once picked it up off his bookshelf and started thumbing through it, but then I started laughing at one part I was reading, and I know he was really pissed at me, like really pissed. . . . Oh, and one time, he, like, ran out of Kleenex, and I yelled at him for running out of Kleenex. I mean, what

*She recounts this story as though she is out with a friend, trying to entertain. Often, she could be quite funny, using humor as a way of downplaying painful feelings (such as hurt), conveying a bit of a "tough" persona as well. In this way, she uses minimization (see Chapter 1) as a means of coping.*

kind of therapist runs out of Kleenex? Doesn't that violate some kind of therapy *law* or something? [laughs]

***R.M.:*** What was that like for you, when he ran out of Kleenex?

***Madeline:*** Well, it was mostly funny. The only time I cry in front of the guy, literally the *one and only* time, and he goes ahead and runs out of Kleenex. I mean, I'm sniffling, and blubbering, and stuff. And wiping my nose on my sleeve. . . . I think I grossed him out.

***R.M.:*** The one and only time you cried in front of him?

***Madeline:*** Yeah. I see the guy for a whole year, I cry once. And then I leave his office all red in the face that day, and it was really embarrassing because, of all times, this is the one my dad chooses to come and pick me up. And my dad looks up from reading his magazine and makes some sarcastic comment about me finally getting everything off my chest. And I thought to myself, "How the fuck did you *know*?"

***R.M.:*** How did he know . . . what?

***Madeline:*** How did he know . . . like, that I was talking about him and all that stuff the whole time. I swear, it's as though he had these radar-like ears that could hear through everything, and he must have known all that shit I was saying about him.

***R.M.:*** What do you remember saying about him?

*Note the double-edged sword inherent in idealization (see Chapter 1). She both admires her father and fears him. Admiration is seen more clearly later in the session, but here as well with "could hear through everything." Of course, the fear (tinged with paranoia) in that phrase is evident as well.*

***Madeline:*** [pause]. Uhm, I don't know. . . . I think it must have been pretty bad though. My voice was raised during the session, but I kinda only realized how loud it had been when I went out into the waiting room and saw my dad sitting there, and how quiet everything seemed then . . . [voice trails off].
[pensive, 10 seconds, looks up at me].
***R.M.:*** What were you thinking about just now?
***Madeline:*** Uhm. . . . I don't know . . . that . . . it was so embarrassing.
***R.M.:*** [nods] Mmm. It sounds embarrassing.
***Madeline:*** Yeah. Like, him seeing me cry and stuff. . . . It was embarrassing enough to be there in the first place.
***R.M.:*** What was hard about him seeing you cry?
***Madeline:*** Uhm . . . uh . . . like, it's not something normal.
***R.M.:*** [nods] Mmm. Okay. Crying makes you feel like you're not normal.
***Madeline:*** Uhm . . . yeah. I mean, it's just so embarrassing. Like, having either of them see me cry. . . . I never cry. I look like an idiot when I do. I mean . . . I used to cry a lot when I was little. Well . . . probably no more than typical kids. But kids cry a lot. You know? I babysat my cousin, and Christ, she cries constantly. It really gets under your skin when they do.

*Note that at this point, 5 months into the therapy, she is able to use silence productively (see Chapter 3). This was not always the case. She had to grow into it within the therapeutic relationship, and I had to "let her" grow into it by not rescuing her from the discomfort silence arouses.*

*Also in this section, crying provokes feelings of embarrassment and humiliation and a sense of vulnerability. The expression of such sentiments raises fear that there is something wrong with her (as seen next).*

***R.M.:*** Hmm. And, it's important to you to feel like there's nothing wrong with you, to feel normal.
***Madeline:*** Yeah. I mean, yeah. Like, I . . . I just didn't want to make such a *big deal* out of it. Like, I made a promise the last time he ever touched me that I would never let myself get so fucked up about it again.
***R.M.:*** How did you get fucked up about it?
***Madeline:*** Uhm . . . like . . . like, with my dad, you know? It kinda got me fucked up, like I would cry about it. But . . . uhm . . . it's also . . . like, when I cry, I also tend to say everything more freely, and uh, just like, a couple months ago, when I first accused my dad of touching me, I was in tears. I don't think I would have confronted him if I hadn't been crying. But I was crying, and although all I could hear in my mind was . . . uh . . . I just had this urge to just go in and confront him, sort of, like I was on autopilot. And it just got so overwhelming, and when I told him what I wanted to say, I was crying then, too. If I hadn't been crying, I think he would have taken it all a little differently.

*Interestingly, she turns crying into a strength. While this could be seen, to some extent, as defensive, it is also part of her wish to adopt a new definition of self that is beginning to emerge through therapy, one that is starting to more readily integrate expressions of painful emotions, vulnerability (see Chapter 3), and dependency.*

***R.M.:*** Uh hmm [nods].
***Madeline:*** But I don't, I don't like to, I wouldn't like to say it was on purpose, I don't really feel I did it on purpose.
***R.M.:*** Hmm. . . . And how did crying

help you in that situation with your dad?

***Madeline:*** I think he took me more seriously because if I accused him straight-faced, he might have thought it was just a ploy to, uhm, hurt him, that I was just trying things, to hurt him, because he hurt me greatly by, uh . . . by not respecting my privacy. But I had already been in tears before we got into that subject, and he saw that I was crying for serious reasons, so I guess I must have played on that, I must have played that up. But if I wouldn't have been crying, I don't think I would have said anything to him.

*She feels guilty for having confronted her father, for expressing feelings of anger toward him, and for wishing, in part, to hurt him. She may also feel afraid of the damage anger could cause to her relationship with him, as seen next.*

***R.M.:*** You say you must have "played that up." Are you saying that your crying, your confronting him somehow wasn't real or legitimate?

***Madeline:*** Uhm . . . it was real . . . yeah, but uh . . . uhm . . . [looks down] [silent, 5 seconds]. When I was a kid, when I didn't know what an outcome would be, I would hold back my reactions no matter how strong they were and not say anything. I used to be really quiet and shy in front of people who I didn't know. But with people I did know, I would lash out when I was angry. And, I was actually quite evil, especially to my sister. And uhm, I guess because I felt comfortable enough. So, in a situation where

I don't know the outcome, like what my dad would say to me, how seriously my dad would react to such an accusation, it helped to be crying because I was in a less-rational state, more emotional. And uh . . . That's why it helped.

*She briefly mentions her sister here, in a way that implies underlying feelings of guilt (describes having been "evil" to her sister). Madeline's relationship with her sister becomes important later, as she is motivated to engage in acts of protectiveness on her sister's behalf.*

***R.M.:*** Mmm [nods].

***Madeline:*** And, uhm, yeah, I guess, I don't know, I always look at things from an evolutionary point of view; in that, we have certain emotions to help us to survive, but then again, humans are rational, and I think being rational takes more effort, it's more complex; so I guess, when we're weakened physically or mentally, when we're weak, we resort to less-rational things that are controlled more by emotion.

***R.M.:*** [nods] Uh hmm.

***Madeline:*** [laughs]. Did I go off topic? . . . Like, I always make an effort to be as rational as possible. I actually pride in that, take pride in that. And I know the stereotype is that women are less rational, so I guess, I try to prove the opposite to other people. And it's a more enjoyable state of being for me than being irrational. Being irrational to me is being emotional. Because, for instance, when I go shopping for something, and I want something expensive, I try to separate it from "Do I want it?" or "Do I need it?" And usually, I'm on the impulse

*There is a good deal of intellectualized speech in this section and the next.*

to buy because I want it. So I wait a day, or a week, or a month, and then I figure if I still want it as much as before, then you know. . . . And, like, sometimes it resolves itself as quick as within 5 minutes. I just say, I figure I was trying to convince myself that I needed something, when in fact I just wanted it. And you know, that emotion builds up so quickly. You, like, get the impulse, but you just gotta take a step back and just weigh things out.

***R.M.:*** Mmm [nods]. . . . I'm thinking back to a couple of weeks ago, when you talked about your mom's emotionality in very negative terms, and you talked about your dad's rationality in very glowing terms, and I'm wondering if this is a similar kind of thing that you're talking about.

***Madeline:*** [silent, 5 seconds] Uh . . . well my mom, like my mom would get very emotional about things. She would make decisions based on worry and fear. And whatever her decisions were, or her advice to us was, was usually based on her own fears and worries and her own personal outcomes, like if she wouldn't want me to go somewhere, it wasn't because it was bad for me, it meant that it might worry her. So, she would try to craft it in a way that would get me to stay and not go out with my friends because it would worry her. But she wouldn't say that, she would say something else, like "stay with your sister," or something like that. And, uhm, I learned to see through that and to be skeptical with her. But my dad was usually very straightforward, there was none of that . . . usually . . . none of that bullshit. Like my dad wouldn't have some. . . uh . . . ulterior motive [silent, 5 seconds]. And uhm . . . he—and once I got into the workforce, I noticed that with management versus the employees in the lower ranks, it's kinda like that. They're very much emotional, they fight and bicker with each other, they're like little kids. And they just, they fight over cigarettes. I swear to God, I've seen them fight over cigarettes. Management is more, like straightforward. They don't, they don't come to you for information just to gossip about you, or they're more relaxed, they're more straightforward kind of people. And I saw that analogy between my mom and my dad as well.

***R.M.:*** [nods]. You make that split between your mom and your dad . . . Who are you saying you prefer to be like?
***Madeline:*** Management . . . uhm, like . . . my dad, for sure.
***R.M.:*** You try to be like your dad?
***Madeline:*** Uh huh . . . [nods]. Yeah.
***R.M.:*** You look up to him?
***Madeline:*** . . . Yeah . . . I always have.
***R.M.:*** [nods]. It's interesting . . . and yet it was your dad who made you feel so very uncomfortable sexually. You've referred to him as sexually—
***Madeline:*** —inappropriate.

*She works hard to reject any aspects of her mother's character, seeing her mother as weak and frightened, seeing emotional expressiveness as part and parcel of that weakness. She imagines more power (and therefore more safety) by rejecting the emotional aspects of herself.*

***R.M.:*** Inappropriate, yes, that's the word you've used. Right. How does that play out for you? Here your dad is someone you've looked up to, you've admired, yet what he did was, in your words, sexually inappropriate, so much so that you confronted him about it just a couple of months ago. How does that work?
***Madeline:*** Uhm . . . it works . . . because . . . because I felt that . . . that he was [pause, 5 seconds] all I really had [voice tightens]. Like I didn't get along with the rest of my family, I mean like my extended family, my mom's brothers and sisters and cous-

*Here, she is invited to struggle with the discrepancy between her idealized image of her father and the painful reality of her own story (recall "narrative discrepancies" in Chapter 3). What does her identification with her father say about her? Is this, in part, why she feels like she is "evil" at times? Also, as she acknowledges and considers the reality of her father's behavior toward her, what does that do to their relationship?*

ins, any of them [begins to tear up] besides my dad.

***R.M.:*** [nods] Mmm—

***Madeline:*** —Like, he really *is* a good person. So since he was basically all I had, it was kinda like [pause, 5 seconds] . . . where the, the victim or hostage, usually, befriends the person who has, you know, taken them hostage [pause, 5 seconds]. You learn to live with what you have, and you make the best of it.

***R.M.:*** Mmm . . . [nods] okay—

***Madeline:*** —yeah . . . I guess . . . and, like, I would inhibit myself from saying anything about it to anybody, because I didn't know what the outcome would be. I didn't, I didn't want to lose my dad's love . . . maybe . . . [continues to tear up] because we really did have a great father–daughter relationship going [silent, 10 seconds] . . . I mean, and . . . this year, he's starting to take it out on my sister and making her really frustrated about her schoolwork, being really hard on her [recomposes herself]. I think it's mostly because he can't control my mother, and he can't get rid of my mother, so he has to control us. And it was just . . . every time he would touch me, I felt I could tolerate it less and less.

*As her defenses are lowered, she begins to express intense anger toward her father, recounting stories she would usually keep hidden (as seen in the next section).*

***R.M.:*** [nods]. Mmm . . .

***Madeline:*** Which is why I'm glad I moved out. I mean, no one could ever come into my house. I used to feel uncomfortable bringing friends to my house, obviously, because my parents acted weird toward them. Actually, my dad was very rude to my sister's friends, to the point where my sister was extremely ticked off, and I told my dad off about it. Like, a few months ago, my sister and her friends were hanging out in the basement, her friends had just slept over, and in the morning, my dad wanted to go out for breakfast, it was a Saturday morning. And he just comes and goes, "Okay guys, get out! We're going for breakfast." And they all look up at each other like, "What the hell's going on. Is this guy just kicking us out?" And uh, yeah [silent, 5 seconds]. And I have, sort of, this uhm . . . well I guess, a memory from my childhood, and I remember that I invited a bunch of people for my birthday [voice quivers], I invited practically the whole class, and only one person came, this girl who used to take the bus with me to school, but like, that's it.

***R.M.:*** [nods]. Mmm.

***Madeline:*** And the rest of the popular girls and everybody else didn't come [chokes up]. Uhm, so—

***R.M.:*** —Mmm . . . that must have been painful.

***Madeline:*** Yeah . . . it was . . . [voice quivering] and through high school, I hardly ever had people over at my house. And right now, I wanna have a party, it's going to be my birthday soon, and I'm having anxieties about people not showing up [tears up]. . . .

***R.M.:*** Mmm. . . . You're looking like you're choking back tears . . . what are you feeling right now?

***Madeline:*** [cries]. It's not like it's negative. It's just overwhelming [cries, 5 seconds].

***R.M.:*** You're feeling overwhelmed. . . .

***Madeline:*** . . . and frustrated.

***R.M.:*** [nods] Mmm. . . .

***Madeline:*** It also like—

***R.M.:*** —Uh hum—

***Madeline:*** —Like, at the time, I felt really rejected.

***R.M.:*** You did [nods], yeah. . . .

***Madeline:*** [cries] Yeah . . . [silent 10 seconds, recomposes herself]. That's why I'm really glad I have Candice. Because she usually has people over, and when I see her, sometimes there's like 50 people at her house, and I just get to talk to different people and socialize [pause]. . . . And I always wonder, I always try to do the best, my best to prevent my sister from going through the same things as I did. She's doing really well, with friends right now, she used to have trouble, but I think she should be okay.

*Accessing feelings of rejection is very painful for her. She only stays there for a little while. Yet, even expressed briefly, this is very different for her. She responds well to being asked what she was feeling right then (see Chapters 4 and 5).*

***R.M.:*** Yeah . . . your sister, you help her? You protect her?

***Madeline:*** Yeah, I do. I try to.

***R.M.:*** That's important to you, to protect her.

***Madeline:*** Yeah . . . [silent, 10 seconds]. It is . . . [pause].

*As mentioned, Madeline is motivated to engage in acts of protectiveness (see Chapter 3) on her sister's behalf. This becomes quite useful in therapy in regard to helping Madeline look inward, as we see in the next section.*

*R.M.:* What were you thinking about just then?
*Madeline:* Just . . . my sister [trails off, silent 5 seconds]. . . . About her standing up to . . . [voice trails off]
*R.M.:* Mmm.
*Madeline:* And about going home to check up on her. Not that she needs it, she's 19. . . . I'm going to swing by after this session. I think, I think I should see her.
*R.M.:* I wonder what it would have been like if there had been someone looking out for you, the way you do now for your sister.
*Madeline:* [silent, 10 seconds]. [very quietly] I don't know. [silent, 5 seconds].
*R.M.:* What do you imagine?
*Madeline:* Uhm [pause]. I don't know. Maybe . . . I don't know. Maybe things would have turned out different. . . . Maybe someone would have told my dad to stop. . . . Maybe . . . [cries] . . . I wouldn't have been such a crazy woman all those years with Kevin.
*R.M.:* [nods]. Mmm . . .
*Madeline:* [cries, recomposes herself] [pensive silence, 10 seconds].
*R.M.:* What were you crying about just now?
*Madeline:* Uhm . . . I'm not sure. . . . Uh, I guess I still get upset when I think about Kevin.
*R.M.:* [nods]. Hmm. Yeah.
*Madeline:* Fuck! Jesus Christ, I've used up half your Kleenex box [laughs].

***R.M.:*** No problem . . . you needed to cry . . . but, I was wondering what this session has been like for you. You know, at the beginning you talked about sometimes feeling so embarrassed crying in front of the therapist you used to see, and your feelings about crying in front of your father. . . . How has it been for you to cry in front of me?
***Madeline:*** Uhm . . . uh, good—uhm. . . . I don't know. I'm not sure.
***R.M.:*** Hmm . . . you're not sure how you feel about it?
***Madeline:*** Yeah, I mean, I don't know. . . . I guess it's kinda weird.
***R.M.:*** [nods]. Right, of course, I imagine it would be. . . . And you may have a lot of different feelings about it over the next week, some good, and some not so good.
***Madeline:*** Yeah. Uhm, yeah . . . okay [silent].
***R.M.:*** Okay. But we need to stop there for today.
***Madeline:*** Yeah. [silent, 5 seconds], okay [looks recomposed].
***R.M.:*** Okay, see you next week, Madeline.

*Her earlier comment about crying in front of her previous therapist (who lacked the requisite Kleenex) has a bearing on her therapeutic relationship with me (see Chapter 5). Will I be able to support her as she cries, or will I fail her as her previous therapist seemed to? Also, appearing vulnerable with me has the mixed effect of both strengthening the relationship and creating anxiety and potential humiliation. Debriefing together can be used to look at what feelings of vulnerability and dependency provoke in the here and now of the therapeutic relationship.*

Madeline continued in therapy, once a week, for about a year and a half, with the ending precipitated by an out-of-town job offer she received on graduating from her business program. By and large, her progress remained consistent, including steady symptomatic improvement, although she did go through periods that were challenging for both of us. For example, termination proved to be somewhat difficult, as avoidant patterns that had diminished seemed to reappear to a certain extent. Nevertheless, even these reappearances were relatively limited in scope, and although she rescheduled the final session twice, she was able to tolerate it and use it productively when we finally did end, expressing sadness over the loss of therapy, along with a certain reflectiveness about the changes made through the treatment process.

In the next chapter, we look at some of the difficulties that arise as treatment comes to a close. As was the case for Madeline, who did make good progress throughout the course of therapy, for individuals in this clinical population, endings can be unpredictable and challenging.

CHAPTER 8

# Ending Therapy

What is the end point in the therapeutic relationship? How does treatment come to a close? "How much is enough?" (Murdin, 2000). When working with clients who are motivated to disengage from intimate relationships to begin with, how do decisions around ending get made? And, how can such individuals even bring themselves to say good-bye?

As has often been said, planning for the ending should occur from the very beginning. It is critical that termination not be something that sneaks up on therapist and client. Nowhere is this more important than when working with individuals who struggle with the closeness inherent in the psychotherapy relationship. Practically speaking, Clarkin, Yeomans, and Kernberg (1999) suggested that, in any extended therapy, there should be a minimum 3-month termination period during which the decision to end is arrived at jointly by client and therapist. And, for treatments lasting several years, the authors suggested a minimum 6-month period.

In the section to follow, we begin to look at termination in more detail, starting with some general principles and guidelines, followed by a problem that is quite common among individuals in this clinical population, that is, premature termination. Finally, we look at therapist feelings that arise around termination and their effects on the treatment.

## General Principles of Termination

A set of guidelines for ending psychotherapy was put forward by Leslie Greenberg (2002), in which he described eight principles for this phase of treatment.[1] These guidelines represent a thoughtful approach to termination that is attentive to the therapeutic relationship, values collaborativeness, and gives the client occasion to examine the very real loss associated with ending therapy.

In Greenberg's (2002) view, first termination is *collaborative*. The individual's emerging decision to end therapy is a critical part of the termination process. In this view, the client is an active agent and is considered the "primary determiner" of when to end. It should be added that the individual's wish to end is often communicated indirectly. Langs (1988) suggested that the therapist is in a position to reflect such indirect communications back to the person, giving the client a sense of permission to think more explicitly about ending and, in time, to jointly set a specific termination date. In Greenberg's second principle, termination is seen as a *choice point* rather than as attainment of an absolute end point. Client improvement and decreasing motivation suggest the end is drawing near. Similarly, Wachtel (2002) underscored the importance of the therapist respecting the individual's choice to end, without expecting the person to achieve a certain predetermined level of functioning before considering termination. Greenberg's third principle considers termination to be a *process of separation*. Feelings of loss are normally expected to arise from separations. The presence and absence of loss-related reactions are meaningful. Some theorists (e.g., Clarkin et al., 1999) have stressed the importance of working on the psychological meaning of termination from the beginning of treatment by discussing the client's reactions to a number of separations from the therapist, including vacations and illnesses.

The fourth principle described by Greenberg (2002) is related to client empowerment. Changes in the direction of goal attainment, or of improved psychological health, should be *attributed to client efforts*. In a similar vein, Wachtel (2002) emphasized the importance of the client owning change not only during the termination phase but also throughout the process of treatment

1. Although Greenberg presented these principles as a way of speaking to termination of experiential therapy in particular, Wachtel's (2002) analysis of current approaches to ending psychotherapy concluded that Greenberg's principles generally reflected sound therapeutic practice regardless of treatment modality.

in general. Greenberg's fifth principle considers termination to be a *time to consolidate new meanings* developed during therapy. Important themes and areas of change are reviewed. In doing so, change is viewed relatively and progressively rather than as some sort of absolute. This opens the door to future work and gives permission for the individual to feel that the potential emergence of old patterns need not imply inadequacy or failure. Thus, the sixth principle described by Greenberg views termination as a *time to create realistic expectations* about change and suggests that the therapist predict occasional relapses as an expected part of the process. In this regard, it is helpful to ask the client to anticipate and examine potential feelings and reactions were a relapse to occur.

Greenberg's (2002) final two principles are more suggestions around termination than principles per se. He argued first for the tapering down of the final few sessions to once every 2 weeks or to once a month, and second for an ending that leaves the door open to future treatment. As new problems or developmental challenges arise, the client should feel permitted by the therapist to consider reconnecting for future consultation as needed without an undue sense of having failed. Interestingly, Curtis (2002) suggested that when a treatment relationship has been long or intense, the therapist might consider letting the client know that she would be pleased to hear from him at some future point in time, such as by correspondence. In this way, the clinician communicates an openness to future interaction.[2]

Although the prospect of future consultations represents somewhat of a departure from more traditional approaches to termination, Wachtel made the case for seeing the process of ending as occurring more flexibly and less as a "once-and-for-all event" (2002, p. 376). Clients can sometimes progress further in treatment at a later point in time as life changes occur: as developmental milestones of adulthood are successfully or unsuccessfully negotiated, as losses or medical illnesses happen, as new difficulties emerge in dealings with aging parents or troubled children, or as other unforeseen emotional challenges arise.

2. In discussing the topic of offering subsequent contacts following termination, Walsh (2007) noted that sometimes the offer of future sessions may be used to manage mixed feelings on the part of the therapist about ending the therapeutic relationship. Walsh viewed this as a kind of avoidance or denial of termination. Clearly, anxieties and personal reactions to separation on the clinician's part can play a pivotal role in decisions made about how to end. Therapist countertransference in termination is discussed later in this chapter.

## Premature Termination

When we see a sense of mutuality and shared goals between therapist and client, the guidelines presented above can be fairly straightforward to implement. As noted, they represent an approach to termination that values such matters as collaborativeness in treatment, the therapeutic relationship, and the importance of reflecting on the loss associated with separations and endings. To the extent that these principles are mutually shared between therapist and client or that they become so over the course of psychotherapy, the termination phase may be no more challenging than any other stage of treatment.

Sometimes, however, things do not unfold so neatly. The term *premature termination*[3] refers to the therapy that ends well before it should. As noted in this chapter, the attempt to terminate prematurely is common among clients in this population as such individuals are motivated to disengage from intimate relationships to begin with.

Premature endings are often abrupt or rushed, lack a sense of completeness, and are unsatisfying for therapist and client alike. In a treatment that has gone on for awhile, termination announcements that come "out of the blue" can be disorienting to the clinician. Sometimes, the individual will decide unilaterally to drop out of therapy without giving notice at all. Or, he may give notice by sending an e-mail or by leaving a late-night voice mail message at a time guaranteed to miss the therapist. Premature terminations have been considered by some (e.g., Greenspan & Kulish, 1985) to be resource wasteful, particularly when they represent a litany of psychotherapy false starts. Importantly, 20–57% of outpatients unilaterally decide to terminate after completing only the first session (Brogan, Prochaska, & Prochaska, 1999).

Perhaps it is somewhat odd to refer to such endings in psychotherapy as premature. The language suggests that there is a certain gold standard regarding treatment length, or regarding symptomatic recovery and problem resolution. The use of *premature* to describe precipitous client-initiated endings may also be thought to diminish the individual's self-determination and autonomy. After all, did we not just get through saying that the client was the "primary determiner" (Greenberg, 2002) of when to end?

However, premature termination can be a useful concept when placed in

3. Here, I focus on premature termination that is client-initiated.

the context of long-standing patterns of relating. To the extent that such patterns are enacted within the therapeutic relationship, the decision to terminate prematurely may, at times, be as much a product of client avoidance, as an authentic expression of client will. The intensity of the therapeutic relationship can be frightening. And discomfort over developing closeness, fear of expressing strong emotions, and the potential for conflict within the relationship can give rise to client avoidance.

For individuals in this clinical population, the wish to terminate precipitously can be a demonstration of the kinds of distancing maneuvers described in earlier chapters (see Chapter 5). Recall that empirical investigations have documented how such clients struggle with closeness in the therapeutic relationship (Daniel, 2006) and put psychological distance between themselves and the clinician. In a study of outpatients in trauma therapy, Kanninen et al. (2000) looked at the therapeutic relationship over the course of treatment and found the ending to be particularly difficult on trauma survivors classified as avoidant of attachment. The authors explained that individuals coped with the impending separation by distancing themselves from their therapist.

To listen fully to our clients means listening to the different mixed feelings that they bring to the table. Expressions of readiness to end often come with mixed feelings and varying motivations. The therapist can be facilitative when encountering the prospect of a premature termination by listening fully, clarifying affect, and helping the individual make meaning of what may be contradictory motivations in relation to wanting to end. In a sense, the therapist's role around such terminations is not that different than it is elsewhere in the treatment.

Still, at the end of the day, thinking about the client's motivations to end and encouraging the individual to think about such motivations himself will only go so far. If the client is inclined to end the relationship, then his wish to terminate must be respected. Davis (2008), discussing the issue of premature termination, underscored this point and cautioned against pressuring a client to continue in therapy. The author noted that:

> Clinical discretion is important in determining the right amount of follow-up effort based on the client, the circumstances, and the severity of the client's problems. . . . The provider has to find the appropriate

> balance between reasonable and caring efforts and what could be construed as unnecessary, intrusive or inappropriate efforts. At some point, it can be concluded that the *client* has abandoned therapy. (p. 181)

### *Presentations of Premature Termination*

There are a few different ways that premature termination looks in practice. One of the classic patterns discussed in the psychotherapy literature has been referred to as *flight into health*. Although the term's specific origin remains unclear, with some theorists (e.g., Bergler, 1949) attributing it to Sigmund Freud, it is known that the concept clearly derives from psychoanalytic theory and has been adopted by other treatment modalities as well (Frick, 1999). It refers to the tendency for some individuals to recover so quickly from troubling symptoms or problems that the therapist is left with the distinct impression that the more difficult or painful work has been avoided. In this view, the client convinces himself that all is now well. Yet, true problem resolution and emotional understanding have been evaded.

With clients who come to therapy when underlying trauma-based issues have sparked some interpersonal or symptomatic difficulty in the here and now, there can be a temptation to end treatment when, after a few sessions, the current crisis has passed. Malan (1979, 1995) pointed out that the "flight" is into apparent, fleeting health. And, unresolved trauma-related conflicts will give rise to further difficulties down the road. In a theoretical analysis of the phenomenon, Frick (1999) noted that the concept of flight into health has tended to be used somewhat pejoratively in the literature, perhaps assuming culpability within the client, often failing to look at the therapist's role in creating the conditions for premature termination to occur.

Premature termination can also be seen in those circumstances when the client experiences *anxiety over dependency*. As detailed throughout this book, feelings of closeness to the therapist can be threatening and can give rise to an uncomfortable sense of intimacy and corresponding feelings of vulnerability. Novick and Novick (2006) considered such conflict around dependency to stem from the client's fear that he may never want to leave. To restore a more familiar level of distance and independence, the individual may feel compelled to end therapy, despite perhaps being in the early stages of the process or despite having started to make some progress on treatment goals. Novick and Novick wrote: "The fear is that they will lose themselves if they can't separate, and therefore they have to leave quickly" (2006, p. 44).

Another way that premature termination looks in practice can be referred to as *turning the tables*. Recall the case of the retired high school teacher presented in Chapter 6, the client who "job interviewed" me in the first session, reading a list of questions off her clipboard, ticking them off as she went. Recall also how she needed to retain control as a way of managing her feelings about starting therapy. In Malan's (1979, 1995) analysis of psychological processes related to premature termination, the author explained that when clients turn the tables in this way, when they make attempts to retain control of the treatment process, there is often a tendency to want to *leave* rather than run the risk of *being left*. Thus, the individual may drop out of therapy early on in the process as a way of *avoiding rejection*.

With clients in this population, there can be a profound sense of pain that goes along with criticism, rejection, and feeling unloved, a pain that most commonly goes unexpressed. Risking future rejections by trusting the clinician and letting the therapeutic relationship become meaningful can be too frightening to bear. Novick and Novick (2006) emphasized the imagined risk of rejection as a powerful factor in the decision some individuals make to end treatment early.

Finally, *external factors* may also have a relevant impact on premature termination and the ways it presents itself in practice. While it may be the case that in any given situation a precipitous ending may be a reflection of various avoidant coping processes, it is worth noting that a number of external influences may also be playing a genuine role in the client's decision on whether to continue with treatment. These factors may include financial changes in the family, job losses, moving, completion of training programs, and so on. It is important not to minimize the relevance of such factors as compared to more internal psychological processes.

One important external influence is that of finances and paying for treatment. The practical limitation imposed by the reality of paying for sessions means that clients, particularly those who feel less secure in their financial stability, sometimes feel compelled to bring an end to treatment sooner than may be advisable from the standpoint of healing or recovery. In addition, therapists working in revenue-generating clinics may make decisions, even unwittingly, that are colored by personal gain. For example, anxieties surrounding "replacing" a client who is considering terminating may be a factor motivating a clinician to keep a case longer than necessary.

However, in the context of a therapeutic relationship that has been the subject of examination throughout the treatment process, conflicts arising from fees and similar external pressures would be, presumably, addressed directly and understood in relation to ongoing themes relevant to a given client. For example, if the individual is, say, suddenly expressing concerns over fees or scheduling as a way of avoiding something important and painful, this would be brought into the room and addressed directly (as with any other issue).

Where external factors become particularly insidious is where they represent the impositions of third parties. The limited health care benefits that some individuals bring to treatment, and the corresponding limit to the number of therapy sessions available, mean that factors external to client, therapist, and the therapeutic relationship become highly relevant to termination planning. Wachtel (2002) noted just how much the ending of psychotherapy is currently influenced by such factors:

> These days, termination often has an integrative dimension I wish it did not have—it integrates the clinical and human needs of the patient with the economic needs of insurance company executives. . . . In proceeding to consider how termination should be approached, I am all too aware of how often the third party in the decision is someone in an office tower who could not care less. (pp. 373–374)

### *Making Premature Termination Less Likely*

As stated, the therapist should adopt the attitude that it is the client's decision to continue or discontinue psychotherapy. However, a precipitous ending is generally as unsatisfying for the client as it is for the clinician. In the early stages of treatment, when asked to review any other therapies in which they may have taken part, individuals whose previous treatments have ended in confusing, incomplete ways often feel uncomfortable or awkward talking about them. They may not be able to say why or how they ended. And, feelings of guilt or rejection (which often go unexpressed) or a sense that there was some misunderstanding may color client perceptions of these previous therapies altogether. Premature termination may represent not only a reenactment of other confusing, painful, or dissatisfying relational endings across the person's life but also a missed opportunity for something different.

So whenever possible, it is much better to aim for a mutually agreed-on termination process. And, although there can be no guarantees, it is certainly possible to make it *less likely* that a premature termination will occur. However, doing so really does mean being attentive to the ending right from the beginning. For example, in the first session or two, when reviewing prior treatments, it is often helpful to ask the client how she imagines *this* therapy ending. How might it be different? Why would she *want* it to be different?

More to the point, when the therapy *means* something to the client, so does its termination. Premature termination becomes much less likely when the client becomes clearer on her *motivation* for treatment. Several studies have demonstrated the important role that client motivation plays in premature termination (Brogan et al., 1999; Greenspan & Kulish, 1985). When we discussed the earlier stages of treatment (in Chapter 3), we looked at ways to clarify client motivation, how to use symptoms early on to help with initial buy-in, how to connect symptoms to broader attachment-related issues, and so on. We saw how the therapist invites the client to reflect on her *reasons* for taking on a process like therapy, given that it often raises uncomfortable, difficult feelings, and how to gently challenge the individual on her initial articulation of treatment goals, asking her to consider what the imagined change would mean to her. Recall, for example, that with the client whose goals are initially stated in global, impressionistic ways like, "I don't want to be so negative all the time," it is important that the clinician take it a few steps further. What is in it for her to "stop being so negative"? What might she gain, and what might she lose? And then, why stick with something like therapy if it makes you talk about the negative things in life?

Client motivation is relevant not only at the beginning stages, but also throughout the course of therapy. At multiple points along the way, it is useful to ask the individual what she is getting out of the process right now. If the crisis has passed, if symptoms have abated, what are we working on currently? When clients are encouraged to articulate treatment goals or objectives, and when they come to see a meaningful connection between those goals and the treatment process, they feel a much stronger sense of *ownership* of the therapy, and premature terminations become much less likely.

As noted, when the therapy means something to the client, so does its termination. In addition to focusing on client motivation, another way the therapist can help make premature termination less likely is by paying attention to the *therapeutic relationship*. This is a point emphasized in both clinical (Basch, 1980) and empirical (Tryon & Kane, 1995) writing on the topic. In Chapter 5, we looked at the therapeutic relationship with individuals in this clinical population and saw how these clients may struggle with a sense of vulnerability that comes with connection to the therapist and how they may use acts of distancing to restore equilibrium. Such retreats can come in the form of comments or behaviors that dismiss or pull back from the therapy. We looked at how important it is for the clinician not to act on these comments and behaviors and instead *make use* of distancing maneuvers in the service of the therapy, particularly by addressing the process occurring between therapist and client in the here and now.

The opening up of a relationship, along with the expression of emotion (without that relationship falling apart), is an unusual experience in the client's life. Through successive interactions that pave the way for more expressive and open contact, the individual can come to feel less threatened by the different feelings that accompany interpersonal closeness. When clients who have difficulty with trust and intimacy have had the chance to look at their feelings and reactions in the immediacy of the therapeutic relationship, it can have a strong impact on their sense of *valuing* the therapy. Here also they come to feel a much stronger sense of owning the process, and premature terminations become less likely.

## Therapist Feelings and Termination

### *Therapist Anxiety: Hanging on to the Client*

The ending of psychotherapy can be hard on the clinician and can raise many different emotions depending on the therapist's personal history. If there has been a palpable change in client functioning, if there has been a deepening of the therapeutic relationship throughout treatment, the clinician may struggle with many complicated feelings around termination. As Dalenberg (2000) pointed out, the sharing of a traumatic burden can intensify the therapeutic connection. With individuals in this clinical population, there is a gratifying feeling that comes with seeing client growth and development, seeing greater client openness and willingness to trust. The sense of "having gone through a lot together" is one that is meaningful to client and therapist alike and can make it difficult to let go of the relationship. Lindy and Wilson (2001) emphasized this point:

> The closeness which develops in the successful treatment of patients with PTSD [post-traumatic stress disorder], like the attachment of fellow survivors, is one that is lasting and also gratifying. Therapists feeling that their treatment should continue indefinitely may be experiencing a positive attachment countertransference resistance to termination. (p. 442)

Clinicians may feel a sense of anxiety about ending with a particular client or about endings in general. Such feelings can lead to a kind of acting out in which the therapist *hangs on* to the case longer than she should. In describing therapist response to termination, Kramer noted that "unconscious emotional, and sometimes economic, dependency of the practitioner upon the patient is one of the most significant complications in the termination process" (1986, p. 529).

Therapist anxiety about ending, or *termination anxiety*, represents a certain emotional difficulty dealing with loss, specifically the loss surrounding the ending of treatment. As many theorists have pointed out, the termination phase of psychotherapy is comparable to the process of separation, loss, and mourning. Difficulties surrounding the impending *loss of the therapeutic relationship* can play a pivotal role in how the clinician negotiates this final stage of treatment. As described, the literal loss of the relationship can be difficult on the therapist, particularly when the work has been meaningful, shared, and rewarding.

However, as pointed out by Martin and Schurtman (1985), there is also an important *loss of professional role* at termination. There comes a time when the client no longer needs us as he once did, or at least he perceives it that way. Either way, unless we can tolerate the hurt that goes along with no longer being needed in the professional role, we may end up undermining the individual's wish to end. The therapist's need to hold on to the professional role sometimes can be seen in desperate attempts to give "last words of advice" (Schiff, 1962).

Martin and Schurtman noted that "this advice-giving is a final attempt on the part of the therapist to have an effect on the client by leaving him or her with 'at least something of worth'" (1985, p. 95).

Attempts to hang on to the professional role can also be seen in the context of clinician rescue fantasies, so common in the treatment of trauma. Along with a wish to rescue those who have suffered the most is a belief about one's own importance to the process. Lindy and Wilson stated that "we as therapists fall into the seductive trap that we are the only ones who can be of help to a particular survivor/patient" (2001, p. 442), as though no one else could possibly care as we did. Wachtel (2002) similarly argued that clinicians often get lulled into a sense of self-importance regarding certain clients, uncomfortable with giving up this role at the stage of termination. In Wachtel's words:

> Therapy is fundamentally an interpersonal process, and, inevitably, the results achieved are the results for that particular dyad. Even in the best of therapies, something different would have been accomplished had the patient seen a different therapist. (p. 382)

### *Therapist Avoidance: Wanting to Drop the Client*

While there are certain clients we hang on to longer than we should, there are also those we can hardly wait to terminate.[4] As detailed in Chapter 6, in response to uncomfortable feelings, such as the rejection that comes with being dismissed, frustration with defensiveness, or exhaustion when progress is slow, clinicians may respond by disengaging from the therapy, sometimes coming to dislike or even hate working with the person. For example, recall that on those occasions that the client is late, the therapist may catch herself secretly wishing he would not show up at all, almost feeling disappointed when, at last, he arrives. Or, in response to acts of distancing and reluctance to change, the therapist may "write the client off," losing hope in the individual's capacity to improve. In time, the clinician may stop putting effort into the case, amounting to a neglect or abandonment of the process, ultimately letting the therapy just

4. Ethical and medical-legal implications of therapist-initiated premature terminations are detailed in an article by Younggren and Gottlieb (2008).

"fizzle away," without any clear sense of how that happened and why exactly the client is no longer coming for treatment.

Being rid of some clients can bring an enormous sense of relief. Feelings of chronic frustration, hurt, and a sense of incompetence in relation to certain cases may make it difficult to stay committed to the process. *Therapist avoidance* of difficult feelings can lead the clinician to *drop the case* before she should.

Such avoidance may be seen in direct attempts to "dump" the client onto unsuspecting colleagues, first-year trainees, or interns. More commonly, though, it is seen in indirect, subtle ways: failing to return client calls, "forgetting" the client's appointment, letting the client get off too easily when he starts questioning whether therapy is really right for him, or failing to suggest a closing session or termination process. One therapist I supervised a few years back felt so discounted by his client's decision to enter into an inpatient trauma treatment program (contrary to the therapist's advice not to) that he considered barring her from outpatient treatment with him after her discharge from the inpatient program.

While the wish to drop a client may arise from the processes described above, it may also be a product of termination anxiety. Recall that termination anxiety (therapist anxiety about ending) represents a certain emotional difficulty dealing with loss, specifically the loss surrounding the ending of treatment. And, recall also that such anxiety can lead to a kind of acting out in which the therapist *hangs on* to the client longer than she should. However, termination anxiety itself can lead to a defensive response in which the therapist does just the opposite (Martin & Schurtman, 1985), essentially *dropping* the client before she should.

As feelings surface, such as hurt and anger over the prospective loss of the client, or as feelings of anxiety are triggered by personal difficulties with separation, the clinician may make attempts at emotional suppression. She may become emotionally unavailable (Kramer, 1986) to the client during the termination stage or may hurry the end along as a way of managing the feelings of loss that termination represents. Martin and Schurtman observed that the therapist may attempt to end treatment in order to "leave the client first" (1985, p. 94), to withdraw emotionally before the final sessions, to become reserved and aloof, to lessen the importance and significance of termination, or to unconsciously provoke the client to end treatment early. Any of these patterns may represent attempts to stave off anxiety about ending but may have the effect of hurrying the individual out the door.

With therapists who, themselves, tend to be avoidant of attachment, separations and losses may have always been managed by way of emotional suppression. One such supervisee, who was working on an adolescent mood disorders unit, struggled on and off throughout the treatment of one particularly traumatized teenager, often finding it difficult to bring sessions to any significant level of depth. At one point in supervision, the clinician acknowledged that the client reminded her of herself at that age. As both client and therapist tended to avoid painful topics, sessions usually stuck close to the surface. Nevertheless, over time, the therapy did show some progress, as seen in the client's increasing reliance on the clinician for support as well as a developing willingness to talk more openly.

As termination approached, the therapist really began to struggle. Her internship was coming to a formal end, yet she would be staying on at the agency in a new capacity. Now that there was no longer an externally imposed reason to terminate, the clinician became deeply ambivalent on how to proceed. As she, herself, had struggled with issues of intimacy in her personal life, the prospect of not having an "out" in her relationship with this client began to make her feel quite anxious. At the same time, she would acknowledge feelings of guilt for wanting to end the therapy when there was no real reason to do so. She would sometimes call on avoidant defenses to manage her feelings around termination, seeming (even more often than usual) to miss emotional moments or empathic opportunities and becoming more distant sounding during sessions.

In time, the client began missing appointments and after a 3-week absence, sent an e-mail to the therapist thanking her, but ending treatment because things were "getting so hectic at home." In this way, the clinician's own difficulties with separation, along with her tendency toward emotional suppression, led her to undermine the termination process, leading the client to miss out on an important aspect of treatment.

## Clinical Overview Points

Things to Remember in Relation to Ending Therapy

- Keep termination in mind right from the beginning.
- Follow a comprehensive set of principles. Greenberg's (2002) approach viewed termination as:

  - A collaborative process.
  - A choice point rather than end point.
  - A process of separation and loss.
  - An empowering process, when change is attributed to client-initiated efforts.
  - A time to consolidate new meanings and changes.
  - A time to be realistic about change.
- Adopt a position around termination that:
  - Helps clarify contradictory motivations around wanting to end.
  - Is respectful of the client's wish to end.
- Make premature termination less likely by:
  - Building in client ownership of the treatment process.
  - Clarifying motivation for therapy throughout the treatment process.
  - Attending to the therapeutic relationship throughout the treatment process.
- Recognize instances when you hang on to the client to manage your feelings (e.g., feelings related to loss of therapeutic relationship or professional role).
- Notice your direct or subtle attempts to pull away or drop the case to manage your feelings (e.g., feelings of frustration, hurt, anxiety, or ambivalence).

# Epilogue: A Final Word

This book began with a quotation from Scott Peck's *All-American Boy* (1995). In his poignant memoir, Peck shared his personal traumatic account, found a way to renew a future for himself, and did so against enormous familial, cultural, and religious pressure to keep silent, to continue to pretend. In my introductory comments, I stated that this book asks the question: How do you engage the client who pretends, the client who denies and minimizes the effects of her own cruel past?

Of course, my hope is that this book has shed some light on this question, but as also noted in the introduction, my goal is that the reader, now reaching the end, will be both realistic about the challenges of the work and hopeful about the prospect of change.

While working with clients in this population can be complicated, psychotherapy may well afford these individuals with a chance for productive reappraisal if the clinician finds opportunities to address attachment patterns and challenge defensive processes. Intrafamilial trauma often develops in a climate of troubled attachment and acts to further disrupt attachment. Through a psychotherapeutic process that values focusing on these disrupted attachments and their emotional meanings, the therapist provides a holding environment for the safe exploration of issues that until now have been far too threatening to examine.

It is important to recognize that when such clients begin treatment, there is, in fact, a deeply rooted vulnerability, a hidden hurt, and an underlying yearning for love and care (Sable, 2004) as much as there is an overt insistence on self-reliance, defensiveness, and the minimization of traumatic events. While they have spent many years turning their attention away from the consequences of their difficult histories, this strategy is no longer effective.

The challenge in treatment, then, is in helping such clients find a way to tell a story too painful to speak but too compelling to ignore.

# References

Ainsworth, M. D. S., & Bell, S. M. V. (1970). Attachment, exploration, and separation: Illustrated by the behavior of one-year-olds in a strange situation. *Child Development, 41*, 49–67.

Ainsworth, M. D. S., & Wittig, B. A. (1969). Attachment and exploratory behavior of one-year-olds in a strange situation. In B. M. Foss (Ed.), *Determinants of infant behavior* (Vol. 4, pp. 111–136). London: Methuen.

Alexander, P. C. (1992). Application of attachment theory to the study of sexual abuse. *Journal of Consulting and Clinical Psychology, 60*, 185–195.

Alexander, P. C., & Anderson, C. L. (1994). An attachment approach to psychotherapy with the incest survivor. *Psychotherapy, 31*, 665–675.

Alexander, P. C., Anderson, C. L., Brand, B., Schaeffer, C. M., Grelling, B. Z., & Kretz, L. (1997). Adult attachment and longterm effects in survivors of incest. *Child Abuse and Neglect, 22,* 45–61.

Allen, J. G., Huntoon, J., Fultz, J., Stein, H., Fonagy, P., & Evans, R. B. (2001). A model for brief assessment of attachment and its application to women in inpatient treatment for trauma-related psychiatric disorders. *Journal of Personality Assessment, 76*, 421–447.

American Psychiatric Association. (2000). *Diagnostic and statistical manual of mental disorders* (4th ed., text revision). Washington, DC: Author.

Aron, L. (1996). *A meeting of minds.* Hillsdale, NJ: Analytic Press.

Axline, V. M. (1969). *Play therapy*. New York: Ballantine Books.

Bakermans-Kranenburg, M. J., & van IJzendoorn, M. H. (2009). The first 10,000 adult attachment interviews: Distributions of adult attachment representations in clinical and non-clinical groups. *Attachment and Human Development, 11*, 223–263.

Bartholomew, K., & Horowitz, L. (1991). Attachment styles among young adults: A test of a four-category model. *Journal of Personality and Social Psychology, 61*, 226–244.

Bartholomew, K., & Shaver, P. R. (1998). Methods of assessing adult attachment: Do they converge? In J. A. Simpson & W. S. Rholes (Eds.), *Attachment theory and close relationships* (pp. 25–45). New York: Guilford.

Bartz, J. A., & Lydon, J. E. (2006). Navigating the interdependence dilemma: Attachment goals and the use of communal norms with potential close others. *Journal of Personality and Social Psychology, 91*, 77–96.

Basch, M. F. (1980). *Doing psychotherapy*. New York: Basic Books.

Baumeister, R. F., Exline, J. J., & Sommer, K. L. (1998). The victim role, grudge theory, and two dimensions of forgiveness. In E. L. Worthington Jr. (Ed.), *Dimensions of forgiveness: Psychological research and theological perspective* (pp. 79–106). Randor, PA: Templeton Foundation Press.

Berant, E., Mikulincer, M., & Florian, V. (2001). Attachment style and mental health: A 1-year follow-up study of mothers of infants with congenital heart disease. *Personality and Social Psychology Bulletin, 27*, 956–968.

Bergler, E. (1949). Prognosis in psychotherapy. *Psychoanalytic Review, 36*, 115–122.

Bernier, A., & Dozier, M. (2002). The client-counselor match and the corrective emotional experience: Evidence from interpersonal and attachment research. *Psychotherapy: Theory, Research, Practice, Training, 39*, 32–43.

Bowlby, J. (1969/1982). *Attachment and loss: Vol. 1. Attachment*. New York: Basic Books.

Bowlby, J. (1973). *Attachment and loss: Vol. 2. Separation*. New York: Basic Books.

Bowlby, J. (1979a). *The making and breaking of affectional bonds*. London: Tavistock Publications.

Bowlby, J. (1979b). Psychoanalysis as art and science. *International Review of Psycho-Analysis, 6*, 3–14.

Bowlby, J. (1980). *Attachment and loss: Vol. 3. Loss, sadness, and depression.* New York: Basic Books.

Bowlby, J. (1988). *A secure base.* New York: Basic Books.

Bretherton, I. (1990). Open communication and internal working models: Their role in the development of attachment relationships. In R. A. Thompson (Ed.), *Nebraska Symposium on Motivation, 1988: Socioemotional development* (pp. 57–113). Lincoln: University of Nebraska Press.

Briere, J. (1988). The long-term clinical correlates of childhood sexual victimization. *Annals of the New York Academy of Sciences, 528,* 327–334.

Brogan, M. M., Prochaska, J. O., & Prochaska, J. M. (1999). Predicting termination and continuation status in psychotherapy using the transtheoretical model. *Psychotherapy, 36,* 105–113.

Chance, M. R. A. (1962). An interpretation of some agonistic postures: The role of "cut-off" acts and postures. *Symposium of the Zoological Society of London, 8,* 71–89.

Chu, J. A., Frey, L. M., Ganzel, B. L., & Matthews, J. A. (1999). Memories of childhood abuse: Dissociation, amnesia, and corroboration. *American Journal of Psychiatry, 156,* 749–755.

Clarkin, J. F., Yeomans, F. E., & Kernberg, O. F. (1999). *Psychotherapy for borderline personality.* New York: Wiley.

Cloitre, M. (2008, May). *Psychotherapy for the interrupted life: Treating survivors of childhood abuse.* Invited clinical workshop, Leading Edge Seminars Inc., Toronto, Canada.

Cloitre, M., Cohen, L. R., & Koenen, K. C. (2006). *Treating survivors of childhood abuse: Psychotherapy for the interrupted life.* New York: Guilford Press.

Cohen, J. A., Mannarino, A. P., & Deblinger, E. (2006). *Treating trauma and traumatic grief in children and adolescents.* New York: Guilford Press.

Connors, M. E. (1997). The renunciation of love: Dismissive attachment and its treatment. *Psychoanalytic Psychology, 14,* 475–493.

Crittenden, P. M. (1992). Children's strategies for coping with adverse home environments: An interpretation using attachment theory. *Child Abuse and Neglect, 16,* 329–344.

Crittenden, P. M. (1999). Danger and development: The organization of self-protective strategies. *Monographs of the Society for Research in Child Development, 64,* 145–171.

Courtois, C. A. (1988). *Healing the incest wound: Adult survivors in therapy.* New York: Norton.

Curtis, R. (2002). Termination from a psychoanalytic perspective. *Journal of Psychotherapy Integration, 12*, 350–357.

Dalenberg, C. J. (2000). *Countertransference and the treatment of trauma.* Washington, DC: American Psychological Association.

Daniel, S. I. F. (2006). Adult attachment patterns and individual psychotherapy: A review. *Clinical Psychology Review, 26*, 968–984.

Davies, J. M., & Frawley, M. G. (1994). *Treating the adult survivor of childhood sexual abuse: A psychoanalytic perspective.* New York: Basic Books.

Davila, J., & Levy, K. N. (2006). Introduction to the special section on attachment theory and psychotherapy. *Journal of Consulting and Clinical Psychology, 74*, 989–993.

Davis, D. D. (2008). *Terminating therapy: A professional guide to ending on a positive note.* Hoboken, NJ: Wiley.

Deutsch, H. (1937). Absence of grief. *Psychoanalytic Quarterly, 6*, 12–22.

Dixon, N. F. (1971). *Subliminal perception: The nature of a controversy.* London: McGraw-Hill.

Dozier, M., & Bates, B. C. (2004). Attachment state of mind and the treatment relationship. In L. Atkinson & S. Goldberg (Eds.), *Attachment issues in psychopathology and intervention* (pp. 167–180). London: Erlbaum.

Dozier, M., Cue, K. L., & Barnett, L. (1994). Clinicians as caregivers: The role of attachment organization in treatment. *Journal of Consulting and Clinical Psychology, 62*, 793–800.

Dozier, M., & Kobak, R. R. (1992). Psychophysiology in adolescent attachment interviews: Converging evidence for dismissing strategies. *Child Development, 63*, 1473–1480.

Dozier, M., & Tyrrell, C. (1998). The role of attachment in therapeutic relationships. In J. A. Simpson & W. S. Rholes (Eds.), *Attachment theory and close relationships* (pp. 221–248). New York: Guilford Press.

Eagle, M. (1996). Attachment research and psychoanalytic theory. In J. M. Masling & R. F. Bornstein (Eds.), *Psychoanalytic perspectives on developmental psychology* (pp. 105–149). Washington, DC: American Psychological Association.

Eagle, M. N. (2006). Attachment, psychotherapy, and assessment: A commentary. *Journal of Consulting and Clinical Psychology, 74*, 1086–1097.

Edelstein, R. S. (2007, February). *Avoiding interference: Adult attachment and emotional processing biases.* Invited research colloquium, York University, Toronto, Canada.

Edelstein, R. S., & Gillath, O. (2008). *Avoiding interference: Adult attachment and emotional processing biases. Personality and social psychology bulletin, 34*, 171–181.

Edelstein, R. S., & Shaver, P. R. (2004). Avoidant attachment: Exploration of an oxymoron. In D. Mashek and A. Aron (Eds.), *Handbook of closeness and intimacy* (pp. 397–412). Mahwah, NJ: Erlbaum.

Erdelyi, M. H. (1974). A new look at the new look: Perceptual defense and vigilance. *Psychological Review, 81*, 1–25.

Fairbairn, W. R. D. (1943). The repression and return of bad objects. Reprinted in W.R.D. Fairbairn (1952), *Psychoanalytic studies of the personality* (pp. 59–81). London: Tavistock/Routledge.

Fonagy, P., Leigh, T., Steele, M., Steele, H., Kennedy, R., Mattoon, G., et al. (1996). The relation of attachment status, psychiatric classification, and response to psychotherapy. *Journal of Consulting and Clinical Psychology, 64*, 22–31.

Freud, A., & Burlingham, D. (1974). *Infants without families and reports on the Hampstead Nurseries 1939–1945.* London: Hogarth.

Freyd, J. J. (1996). *Betrayal trauma: The logic of forgetting childhood abuse.* Cambridge, MA: Harvard University Press.

Freyd, J. J. (2001). Memory and dimensions of trauma: Terror may be "all-too-well remembered" and betrayal buried. In J. R. Conte (Ed.), *Critical issues in child sexual abuse: Historical, legal, and psychological perspectives* (pp. 139–173). Thousand Oaks, CA: Sage.

Frick, W. B. (1999). Flight into health: A new interpretation. *Journal of Humanistic Psychology, 39*, 58–81.

Gelinas, D. (1983). The persistent negative effects of incest. *Psychiatry, 46*, 312–332.

Gelso, C. J., & Hayes, J. A. (1998). *The psychotherapy relationship: Theory, research, and practice.* New York: Wiley.

George, C., Kaplan, N., & Main, M. (1996). *Adult attachment interview* (3rd ed.). Unpublished manuscript, Department of Psychology, University of California, Berkeley.

George, C., & Solomon, J. (1996). Representational models of relationships:

Links between caregiving and attachment. *Infant Mental Health Journal, 17*, 198–216.

George, C., & Solomon, J. (1999). Attachment and caregiving: The caregiving behavioral system. In J. Cassidy & P. R. Shaver (Eds.), *Handbook of attachment: Theory, research, and clinical implications* (pp. 649–670). New York: Guilford Press.

George, C., & West, M. (2001). The development and preliminary validation of a new measure of adult attachment: The adult attachment projective. *Attachment and Human Development, 3*, 30–61.

George, C., & West, M. (2004). The adult attachment projective: Measuring individual differences in attachment security using projective methodology. In M. J. Hilsenroth & D. L. Segal (Eds.), *Comprehensive handbook of psychological assessment, Vol. 2: Personality assessment* (pp. 431–447). Hoboken, NJ: Wiley.

Gil, E. (2006). *Helping abused and traumatized children: Integrating directive and nondirective approaches*. New York: Guilford Press.

Gormley, B. (2004). Application of adult attachment theory to treatment of chronically suicidal, traumatized women. *Psychotherapy: Theory, Research, Practice, Training, 41*, 136–143.

Greenberg, L. (2002). Termination of experiential psychotherapy. *Journal of Psychotherapy Integration, 12*, 358–363.

Greenberg, L. (2008). Emotion and cognition in psychotherapy: The transforming power of affect. *Canadian Psychology, 49*, 49–59.

Greenberg, L., & Pascual-Leone, A. (2006). Emotion in psychotherapy: A practice-friendly research review. *Journal of Clinical Psychology: In Session, 62*, 611–630.

Greenspan, M., & Kulish, N. M. (1985). Factors in premature termination in long-term psychotherapy. *Psychotherapy, 22*, 75–82.

Haji, R., McGregor, I., & Kocalar, D. (2005, January). *Avoidants' reactions to attachment affirmations*. Paper presented at the annual meeting of the Society for Personality and Social Psychology, New Orleans.

Hardy, G. E., Stiles, W. B., Barkham, M., & Startup, M. (1998). Therapist responsiveness to client interpersonal styles during time-limited treatments for depression. *Journal of Consulting and Clinical Psychology 66*, 304–312.

Havens, L. (1986). *Making contact: Uses of language in psychotherapy*. Cambridge, MA: Harvard University Press.

Heinicke, C. M., & Westheimer, I. (1966). *Brief separations*. New York: International Universities Press.

Herman, J. L. (1992). *Trauma and recovery: The aftermath of violence from domestic to political terror*. New York: Basic Books.

Hesse, E. (1999). The adult attachment interview: Historical and current perspectives. In J. Cassidy & P. R. Shaver (Eds.), *Handbook of attachment: Theory, research, and clinical applications* (pp. 395–433). New York: Guilford Press.

Higgins, G. O. (1994a, October). *Resilient adults: Overcoming a cruel past*. Paper presented at the meeting of the Society for Family Therapy and Research, Weston, MA.

Higgins, G. O. (1994b). *Resilient adults: Overcoming a cruel past*. San Francisco: Jossey-Bass.

Hilgard, E. R. (1973). A neo-dissociation interpretation of pain reduction in hypnosis. *Psychological Review, 80*, 396–411.

Hilgard, E. R. (1974). Toward a neo-dissociation theory: Multiple cognitive controls in human functioning. *Perspectives in Biology and Medicine, 17*, 301–316.

Hinde, R. A. (*1982*). *Ethology*. New York: Oxford University Press.

Holmes, J. (1997). Attachment, autonomy, intimacy: Some clinical implications of attachment theory. *British Journal of Medical Psychology, 70*, 231–248.

Holmes, J. (1999). Narrative, attachment and the therapeutic process. In C. Mace (Ed.), *Heart and soul: The therapeutic face of philosophy* (pp. 147–161). New York: Routledge.

Holmes, J. (2001). *The search for the secure base: Attachment theory and psychotherapy*. East Sussex, UK: Brunner-Routledge.

Horowitz, M. J. (1976). *Stress response syndromes*. New York: Aronson.

Horowitz, M. J. (2001). *Stress response syndromes* (4th ed.). London: Aronson.

Jorgensen, R. S., Johnson, B. T., Kolodziej, M. E., & Schreer, G. E. (1996). Elevated blood pressure and personality: A meta-analytic review. *Psychological Bulletin, 120*, 293–320.

Kaner, A., & Prelinger, E. (2005). *The craft of psychodynamic psychotherapy*. New York: Aronson.

Kanninen, K., Salo, J., & Punamaki, R. L. (2000). Attachment patterns and working alliance in trauma therapy for victims of political violence. *Psychotherapy Research, 10*, 435–449.

Kramer, S. A. (1986). The termination process in open-ended psychotherapy: Guidelines for clinical practice. *Psychotherapy, 23*, 526–531.

Kuhn, N. S., & McCullough, L. (2002). Short-term dynamic psychotherapy: Resolving character pathology by treating affect phobias. In S. G. Hofman & M. C. Tompson (Eds.), *Treating chronic and severe mental disorders: A handbook of empirically supported interventions* (pp. 403-418). New York: Guilford Press.

Labriola, T. (Producer), Carlson, J. (Moderator), & Kjos, D. (Moderator). (1998). *Object-relations therapy with Drs. Jill and David Scharff* [Film]. Boston: Allyn & Bacon.

Langs, R. (1988). *A primer of psychotherapy*. New York: Gardner Press.

Levy, K. N., Meehan, K. B., Kelly, K. M., Reynoso, J. S., Weber, M., Clarkin, J. F., & Kernberg, O. F. (2006). Change in attachment patterns and reflective function in a randomized control trial of transference-focused psychotherapy for borderline personality disorder. *Journal of Consulting and Clinical Psychology, 74*, 1027–1040.

Lieberman, A. F. (2004). Traumatic stress and quality of attachment: Reality and internalization in disorders of infant mental health. *Infant Mental Health Journal, 25*, 336–351.

Lieberman, M. D., Eisenberger, N. I., Crockett, M. J., Tom, S. M., Pfeifer, J. H., & Way, B. M. (2007). Putting feelings into words: Affect labeling disrupts amygdala activity in response to affective stimuli. *Psychological Science, 18*, 421–428.

Lindy, J. D., & Wilson, J. P. (1994). Empathic strain and countertransference roles: Case illustrations. In J. P. Wilson & J. D. Lindy (Eds.), *Countertransference in the treatment of PTSD* (pp. 62–82). New York: Guilford Press.

Lindy, J. D., & Wilson, J. P. (2001). Respecting the trauma membrane: Above all, do no harm. In J. P. Wilson, M. J. Friedman, & J. D. Lindy (Eds.), *Treating psychological trauma and PTSD* (pp. 432–445). New York: Guilford Press.

Linehan, M. M. (1993). *Cognitive-behavioral treatment of borderline personality disorder*. New York: Guilford Press.

Liotti, G. (2002). Patterns of attachment and the assessment of interpersonal schemata: Understanding and changing difficult patient-therapist relationships in cognitive psychotherapy. In R. L. Leahy & E. T. Dowd (Eds.), *Clinical advances in cognitive psychotherapy: Theory and application* (pp. 377–388). New York: Springer.

Liotti, G. (2004). Trauma, dissociation, and disorganized attachment: Three strands of a single braid. *Psychotherapy: Theory, Research, Practice, Training, 41*, 472–486.

Liotti, G. (2007). Internal working models of attachment in the therapeutic relationship. In P. Gilbert & R. L. Leahy (Eds.), *The therapeutic relationship in the cognitive behavioural psychotherapies* (pp. 143–161). New York: Routledge.

Logue, M. (2006). *Aggressive responses to peer rejection and acceptance as a function of rejection sensitivity and attachment style.* Unpublished master's thesis, York University, Toronto, Canada.

Lorinc, J. (2008, April 29). I solemnly promised to keep the secret. *The Globe and Mail*, p. F10.

Luborsky, L. (1984). *Principles of psychoanalytic psychotherapy: A manual for supportive-expressive treatment.* New York: Basic Books.

Luthar, S. S., Cicchetti, D., & Becker, B. (2000). The construct of resilience: A critical evaluation and guidelines for future work. *Child Development, 71*, 543–562.

Main, M. B. (1977). Analysis of a peculiar form of reunion behaviour in some day-care children: Its history and sequelae in children who are home-reared. In R. Webb (Ed.), *Social development in childhood: Day-care programs and research* (pp. 33–78). Baltimore, MD: Johns Hopkins University Press.

Main, M., Kaplan, N., & Cassidy, J. (1985). Security in infancy, childhood, and adulthood: A move to the level of representation. *Monographs of the Society for Research in Child Development, 50*, 66–106.

Malan, D. H. (1979). *Individual psychotherapy and the science of psychodynamics* (1st ed.). Oxford, UK: Butterworth/Heinemann.

Malan, D. H. (1995). *Individual psychotherapy and the science of psychodynamics* (2nd ed.). Oxford, UK: Butterworth/Heinemann.

Mallinckrodt, B. (2000). Attachment, social competencies, social support, and interpersonal process in psychotherapy. *Psychotherapy Research, 10*, 239–266.

Mallinckrodt, B., Porter, M. J., & Kivlighan, D. M., Jr. (2005). Client attachment to therapist, depth of in-session exploration, and object relations in brief psychotherapy. *Psychotherapy: Theory, Research, Practice, Training, 42*, 85–100.

Martin, E. S., & Schurtman, R. (1985). Termination anxiety as it affects the therapist. *Psychotherapy, 22*, 92–96.

Masterson, J. F. (1985). *The real self: A developmental, self, and object relations approach.* New York: Brunner/Mazel.

Mauss, I. B., & Gross, J. J. (2004). Emotion suppression and cardiovascular disease: Is hiding feelings bad for your heart? In L. R. Temoshok, I. Nyklicek, & A. Vingerhoets (Eds.), *Emotional expression and health: Advances in theory, assessment, and clinical applications* (pp. 62–81). New York: Brunner-Routledge.

McBride, C., Atkinson, L., Quilty, L. C., & Bagby, R. M. (2006). Attachment as moderator of treatment outcome in major depression: A randomized trial of interpersonal psychotherapy versus cognitive behavior therapy. *Journal of Consulting and Clinical Psychology, 74*, 1041–1054.

McCullough, L. (1998). Short-term psychodynamic therapy as a form of desensitization: Treating affect phobias. *In Session: Psychotherapy in Practice, 4*, 35–53.

McCullough, L. (2001). Desensitization of affect phobias in short-term dynamic psychotherapy. In M. F. Solomon, R. J. Neborsky, L. McCullough, M. Alpert, F. Shapiro, & D. Malan (Eds.), *Short-term therapy for long-term change.* New York: Norton.

McCullough, L., & Andrews, S. (2001). Assimilative integration: Short-term dynamic psychotherapy for treating affect phobias. *Clinical Psychology: Science and Practice, 8*, 82–97.

McLewin, L. A., & Muller, R. T. (2006). Attachment and social support in the prediction of psychopathology among young adults with and without a history of physical maltreatment. *Child Abuse and Neglect 30*, 171–191.

Meyer, B., & Pilkonis, P. A. (2001). Attachment style. *Psychotherapy: Theory, Research, Practice, Training, 38*, 466–472.

Mikulincer, M. (1995). Attachment style and the mental representation of the self. *Journal of Personality and Social Psychology, 69*, 1203–1215.

Mikulincer, M., Dolev, T., & Shaver, P. R. (2004). Attachment-related strategies during thought suppression: Ironic rebounds and vulnerable self-representations. *Journal of Personality and Social Psychology, 87*, 940–956

Mikulincer, M., & Florian, V. (1995). Appraisal of and coping with a real-life stressful situation: The contribution of attachment styles. *Personality and Social Psychology Bulletin, 21*, 406–414.

Mikulincer, M., & Florian, V. (1998). The relationship between adult attachment styles and emotional and cognitive reactions to stressful events. In J. A.

Simpson & W. S. Rholes (Eds.), *Attachment theory and close relationships* (pp. 143–165). New York: Guilford Press.

Mikulincer, M., & Florian, V. (2000). Exploring individual differences in reactions to mortality salience: Does attachment style regulate terror management mechanisms? *Journal of Personality and Social Psychology 79*, 260–273.

Mikulincer, M., & Shaver, P. R. (2003). The attachment behavioral system in adulthood: Activation, psychodynamics, and interpersonal processes. In M. P. Zanna (Ed.), *Advances in experimental social psychology* (Vol. 35, pp. 53–152). San Diego, CA: Academic Press.

Miller, W. R., & Rollnick, S. (2002). *Motivational interviewing: Preparing people for change.* New York: Guilford Press.

Mills, J. (2005). *Treating attachment pathology.* Toronto: Aronson.

Modell, A. H. (1975). A narcissistic defence against affects and the illusion of self-sufficiency. *International Journal of Psycho-Analysis, 56*, 275–282.

Mohr, J. J., Gelso, C. J., & Hill, C. E. (2005). Client and counselor trainee attachment as predictors of session evaluation and countertransference behavior in first counseling sessions. *Journal of Counseling Psychology, 52*, 298–309.

Muller, R. T. (2006, June). *Working with dismissing trauma patients: An integrative attachment-based approach.* Invited presentation, Trauma and Resiliency Program, University of Toronto, Toronto, Canada.

Muller, R. T. (2007, November). *Engaging clients who minimize, disconnect, and avoid trauma reactions in treatment.* Invited presentation, Trauma and Resiliency Program, University of Toronto, Toronto, Canada.

Muller, R. T. (2009). Trauma and dismissing (avoidant) attachment: Intervention strategies in individual psychotherapy. *Psychotherapy: Theory, Research, Practice, Training, 46*, 68–81.

Muller, R. T., Bedi, R., Zorzella, K., & Classen, C. (2008, November). *Attachment and therapeutic alliance in psychotherapy: Theoretical and clinical issues.* Paper presented at the 25th annual conference of the International Society for the Study of Trauma and Dissociation, Chicago.

Muller, R. T., Caldwell, R. A., & Hunter, J. E. (1994). Factors predicting the blaming of victims of physical child abuse or rape. *Canadian Journal of Behavioural Science, 26*, 259–279.

Muller, R.T., Kraftcheck, E. R., & McLewin, L. A. (2004). Adult attachment and trauma. In D. R. Catherall (Ed.), *Handbook of stress, trauma, and the family.* New York: Brunner-Routledge.

Muller, R. T., Lemieux, K. E., & Sicoli, L. A. (2001). Attachment and psychopathology among formerly maltreated adults. *Journal of Family Violence, 16,* 151–169.

Muller, R. T., & Rosenkranz, S. E. (2009). Attachment and treatment response among adults in inpatient treatment for posttraumatic stress disorder. *Psychotherapy: Theory, Research, Practice, Training, 46,* 82–96.

Muller, R. T., Sicoli, L. A., & Lemieux, K. E. (2000). Relationship between attachment style and posttraumatic stress symptomatology among adults who report the experience of childhood abuse. *Journal of Traumatic Stress, 13,* 321–332.

Murdin, L. (2000). *How much is enough? Endings in psychotherapy and counselling.* New York: Routledge.

Norman, D. A. (1976). *Memory and attention: Introduction to human information processing* (2nd ed.). New York: Wiley.

Novick, J., & Novick, K. K. (2006). *Good goodbyes: Knowing how to end in psychotherapy and psychoanalysis.* New York: Aronson.

Ogden, P., Minton, K., & Pain, C. (2006). *Trauma and the body: A sensorimotor approach to psychotherapy.* New York: Norton.

Parkes, C. M. (1973). Factors determining the persistence of phantom pain in the amputee. *Journal of Psychosomatic Research, 17,* 97–108.

Pearlman, L. A., & Courtois, C. A. (2005). Clinical applications of the attachment framework: Relational treatment of complex trauma. *Journal of Traumatic Stress, 18,* 449–459.

Pearlman, L. A., & Saakvitne, K. W. (1995). *Trauma and the therapist: Countertransference and vicarious traumatization in psychotherapy with incest survivors.* New York: Norton.

Pearson, J. L., Cohn, D. A., Cowan, P. A., & Cowan, C. P. (1994). Earned- and continuous-security in adult attachment: Relation to depressive symptomatology and parenting style. *Development and Psychopathology, 6,* 359–373.

Peck, S. (1995). *All-American boy.* New York: Scribner.

Perris, C. (2000). Personality-related disorders of interpersonal behaviour: A developmental-constructivist cognitive psychotherapy approach to treatment based on attachment theory. *Clinical Psychology and Psychotherapy, 7,* 97–117.

Peterfreund, E. (1971). Information, systems, and psychoanalysis: An evolutionary biological approach to psychoanalytic theory. *Psychological Issues, 7*(1), 1–397.

Robertson, J. (1952). *A two-year-old goes to hospital* [Film]. London: Tavistock Child Development Research Unit.

Roisman, G. I., Padron, E., Sroufe, L. A., & Egeland, B. (2002). Earned-secure attachment status in retrospect and prospect. *Child Development, 73,* 1204–1219.

Rosenkranz, S. E., Muller, R. T., & Bedi, R. (2007, November). *The role of attachment in treatment outcome for adults undergoing inpatient treatment for PTSD.* Paper presented at the 24th annual conference of the International Society for the Study of Trauma and Dissociation, Philadelphia.

Sable, P. (2000). *Attachment and adult psychotherapy.* London: Aronson.

Sable, P. (2004). Attachment, ethology and adult psychotherapy. *Attachment & Human Development, 6,* 3–19.

Schiff, S. K. (1962). Termination of therapy: Problems in a community psychiatric out-patient clinic. *Archives of General Psychiatry, 6,* 93–98.

Schore, A. N. (2008, November). *Right brain affect regulation: An essential mechanism of development, trauma, dissociation, and psychotherapy.* Plenary paper delivered at the 25th annual conference of the International Society for the Study of Trauma and Dissociation, Chicago.

Shedler, J., Mayman, M., & Manis, M. (1993). The illusion of mental health. *American Psychologist, 48,* 1117–1131.

Shorey, H. S., & Snyder, C. R. (2006). The role of adult attachment style in psychopathology and psychotherapy outcomes. *Review of General Psychology, 10,* 1–20.

Slade, A. (1999). Attachment theory and research: Implications for the theory and practice of individual psychotherapy with adults. In J. Cassidy & P. R. Shaver (Eds.), *Handbook of attachment: Theory, research, and clinical applications* (pp. 575–594). New York: Guilford Press.

Slade, A. (2004). Two therapies: Attachment organization and the clinical process. In L. Atkinson & S. Goldberg (Eds.), *Attachment issues in psychopathology and intervention.* London: Erlbaum.

Solomon, J., George, C., & De Jong, A. (1995). Children classified as controlling at age six: Evidence of disorganized representational strategies and aggression at home and school. *Development and Psychopathology, 7,* 447–464.

Steiner, J. (1993). *Psychic retreats: Pathological organizations in psychotic, neurotic, and borderline patients*. London: Routledge/Taylor & Francis Group.

Stovall-McClough, K. C., & Cloitre, M. (2006). Unresolved attachment, PTSD, and dissociation in women with childhood abuse histories. *Journal of Consulting and Clinical Psychology, 2*, 219–228.

Tansey, M. J., & Burke, W. F. (1989). *Understanding countertransference*. Hillsdale, NJ: Analytic Press.

Target, M., Fonagy, P., & Shmueli-Goetz, Y. (2003). Attachment representations in school-age children: The development of the Child Attachment Interview (CAI). *Journal of Child Psychotherapy, 29*, 171–186.

Tasca, G. A., Balfour, L., Ritchie, K., & Bissada, H. (2007). The relationship between attachment scales and group therapy alliance growth differs by treatment type for women with Binge-Eating Disorder. *Group Dynamics: Theory, Research, Practice, 11*, 1–14.

Taurke, E., McCullough, L., Winston, A., Pollack, J., & Flegenheimer, W. (1990). Change in affect-defense ratio from early to late sessions in relation to outcome. *Journal of Clinical Psychology, 46*, 657–668.

Teitelbaum, S. H. (1999). *Illusion and disillusionment: Core issues in psychotherapy*. New York: Aronson.

Tryon, G. S., & Kane, A. S. (1995). Client involvement, working alliance, and type of therapy termination. *Psychotherapy Research, 5*, 189–198.

Tulving, E. (1972). Episodic and semantic memory. In E. Tulving & W. Donaldson (Eds.), *Organization of Memory*. New York: Academic Press.

Tyrrell, C. L., Dozier, M., Teague, G. B., & Fallot, R. D. (1999). Effective treatment relationships for persons with serious psychiatric disorders: The importance of attachment states of mind. *Journal of Consulting and Clinical Psychology, 67*, 725–733.

van IJzendoorn, M. H., & Bakermans-Kranenburg, M. J. (1996). Attachment representations in mothers, fathers, adolescents, and clinical groups: A meta-analytic search for normative data. *Journal of Consulting and Clinical Psychology, 64*, 8–21.

van IJzendoorn, M. H., & Bakermans-Kranenburg, M. J. (2008). The distribution of adult attachment representation in clinical groups: A meta-analytic search for patterns of attachment in 105 AAI studies. In S. Howard & M. Steele (Eds.), *Clinical applications of the adult attachment interview* (pp. 69–96). New York: Guilford Press.

Wachtel, P. L. (2002). Termination of therapy: An effort at integration. *Journal of Psychotherapy Integration, 12*, 373–383.

Wallin, D. (2007). *Attachment in psychotherapy.* New York: Guilford Press.

Walsh, J. (2007). *Endings in clinical practice: Effective closure in diverse settings* (2nd ed.). Chicago: Lyceum Books.

Wampold, B. E. (2001). *The great psychotherapy debate: Models, methods, and findings.* London: Erlbaum.

Weinfield, N. S., Sroufe, L. A., & Egeland, B. (2000). Attachment from infancy to early adulthood in a high-risk sample: Continuity, discontinuity, and their correlates. *Child Development, 71*, 695–702.

Weiss, J. (1986). The patient's unconscious work. In J. Weiss & H. Sampson (Eds.), *The psychoanalytic process* (pp. 101–116). New York: Guilford Press.

West, M. L., Sheldon, A., & Reiffer, L. (1989). Attachment theory and brief psychotherapy: Applying current research to clinical interventions. *Canadian Journal of Psychiatry, 34*, 369–374.

Wilson, J. P., & Lindy, J. D. (Eds.). (1994). *Countertransference in the treatment of PTSD.* New York: Guilford Press.

Wilson, J. P., Lindy, J. D., & Raphael, B. (1994). Empathic strain and therapist defense. In J. P. Wilson & J. D. Lindy (Eds.), *Countertransference in the treatment of PTSD* (pp. 31–61). New York: Guilford Press.

Winnicott, D. W. (1947). Hate in the countertransference. Reprinted in D. W. Winnicott (1975), *Through paediatrics to psycho-analysis* (pp. 194–203). New York: Basic Books.

Winnicott, D. W. (1960). Ego distortion in terms of true and false self. Reprinted in D. W. Winnicott (1965), *The maturational processes and the facilitating environment: Studies in the theory of emotional development* (pp. 140–152). New York: International Universities Press.

Winnicott, D. W. (1969). The use of an object and relating through identifications. Reprinted in D. W. Winnicott (1971), *Playing and reality* (pp. 86–94). New York: Routledge.

Younggren, J. N., & Gottlieb, M. C. (2008). Termination and abandonment: History, risk, and risk management. *Professional Psychology: Research and Practice, 39*, 498–504.

# Index

*The letter "n" following a page number refers to a footnote.*